D1600191

DAILY COMPANION
FOR MEN

"Arise, take the child and his mother, and flee to Egypt." —Mt 2:13

DAILY COMPANION
FOR MEN

MINUTE MEDITATIONS FOR EVERY DAY
CONTAINING AN INSPIRATIONAL READING,
A REFLECTION, AND A PRAYER

By
Allan F. Wright

CATHOLIC BOOK PUBLISHING CORP.
New Jersey

CONTENTS

NIHIL OBSTAT: Fr. Philip-Michael F. Tangorra, S.T.L.
Censor Librorum

IMPRIMATUR: ✠ Most Rev. Arthur J. Serratelli, S.T.D., S.S.L., D.D.
Bishop of Paterson

June 30, 2017

(T-177)

ISBN 978-1-941243-94-7

© 2017 Catholic Book Publishing Corp., N.J.
Printed in China   21 HA 2
catholicbookpublishing.com

INTRODUCTION

W HEN men encounter Jesus Christ and commit their lives to furthering their relationship with Him, positive change occurs. Men become better husbands, fathers, brothers, priests, and disciples. As followers of Christ they serve not only their families but strengthen the culture and bear witness to God's love and mercy in the world.

No matter where you are in your personal relationship with Christ the fact is that we can always go deeper. Catholic men are called to grow in our faith throughout our life and that process calls for continual, life-long discipleship. Men who are involved in parish men's groups and who are active in their faith community witness to God's love and can be a catalyst for other men to grow in faith.

In our current Catholic culture there is a lack of male leadership for young men in religious education programs and in parishes. Often the biggest excuse men make is that they don't have time which translates as; "It's not important for me."

This book is intentionally designed for men who are busy yet desire to make God a priority in their lives. Most of the reflections begin with either a quote from scripture or a saint, end with a brief prayer, and have a short reflection specifically written to assist men in living out their Catholic faith each day.

Jesus Christ is the model for all spirituality. It is Jesus who is our model in prayer, forgiveness, mercy, evangelization, and living life to the fullest. The same discipline and focus that an elite athlete displays in their preparation, practice, and dedication is similar to that of a Catholic man who puts his faith into action.

As a husband to a wonderful wife and as a father to four children, I have witnessed the positive impact that living a life committed to Jesus has had in my life. I have also witnessed others who were searching for more in life come to faith in Jesus who can give life both meaning and purpose. May this book be an inspiration and a daily reminder of God's love for you and of our responsibility to bring that love into our world.

Allan F. Wright
Feast of St. Joseph
March 19, 2017

EEP alert; stand firm in the faith; be courageous; be strong. Everything that you do should be done in love.

—1 Cor 16:13-14

JAN. 1

Like a soldier on patrol

REFLECTION. St. Paul is writing to a small community which is under attack because of their new found faith. While their first instinct may be to fight, St. Paul suggests another way to respond. This way calls for courage, faith and love.

When opposition comes to you take St. Paul's words to heart and keep alert, stand firm in faith and do all with love.

PRAYER. *Lord Jesus, may I be attentive and loving to the people You place in my life.*

 HOW yourself to them in all respects as a model of good works. —Tit 2:7

JAN. 2

Faith in action

REFLECTION. People may not always hear what you say but they do hear what you do. Another way of saying this is that people would rather see a sermon than to hear one.

In your effort to be the man God has called you to be, be a good model for your children, wife, friends, and even strangers. Today is a good day to begin.

PRAYER. *Jesus, may I follow Your example and be a good example for those in my life.*

7

HEN I was a child, I used to talk like a child, think like a child, and reason like a child. However, when I became a man, I put all childish ways aside. —1 Cor 13:11

JAN.
3

Re-adjusting our vision

REFLECTION. Most religions have ceremonies during the teenage years which mark a young person's entrance into adulthood.

Each person reaches maturity at their own pace. Let us re-orient ourselves to the important things in life.

PRAYER. *Come Holy Spirit, help me release my grip on childish things and be the man You call me to be.*

———————

 UT as for you, man of God, you must shun all this. Rather, pursue righteousness, godliness, faith, love, fortitude, and gentleness. —1 Tim 6:11

JAN.
4

Focus on what is really important

REFLECTION. In professional football there are over 700 rules. It can be easy to get 'bogged down' in the rules and lose focus of the goal.

St. Paul gives his young disciple Timothy some sound advice when it comes to living as a Christian: pursue righteousness, godliness, faith, love, fortitude, and gentleness.

PRAYER. *Heavenly Father, allow me the grace to pursue what is true rather than what is expedient.*

HY do you call me "Lord, Lord," but fail to do what I tell you?

—Lk 6:46

JAN. 5

No lip service needed

REFLECTION. Jesus is not Lord at all if Jesus is not Lord of all.

It's necessary to stake stock in our lives and see if what we say we believe matches up to how we are living. This self-reflection can be humbling but it can set us on a better path. Throughout all the days of our life stand firm in faith before our Lord.

PRAYER. *Lord God, forgive me for those times I have been hypocritical in my actions.*

BRAHAM was the father of Isaac, Isaac the father of Jacob, Jacob the father of Judah and his brothers.

—Mt 1:2

JAN. 6

From father to father

REFLECTION. The genealogy of Jesus is often overlooked as just a series of names of people from antiquity who have little relevance for the modern believer.

We realize that we too have a genealogy and that our father and those who came before him have shaped the man we have become. What traits have you acquired from your ancestors? Which ones do you desire to pass on?

PRAYER. *Heavenly Father, may I exemplify the best of my forefathers and be a good example.*

REPENT, for the kingdom of heaven is close at hand. —Mt 3:2

A change from within

REFLECTION. The first words of John the Baptist in the Gospel of Matthew are an alarming call for action. "Repent!" John the Baptist didn't call together a focus group nor did he call a committee to discuss his evangelization plan. He called people to turn from sin.

Consider John the Baptist's words a wakeup call and reflect on where God wants you to repent.

PRAYER. *Lord, change is difficult but with Your grace all things are possible.*

PRODUCE good fruit as proof of your repentance. —Mt 3:8

A little less talk and a little more action

REFLECTION. When we consider productivity in the business world we see professionals who are results oriented. Often, what motivates their decisions are finances.

Believe it or not, disciples of Jesus are called to be productive too. It's not financial gain which should motivate us but rather acts of mercy, kindness, and love which are the "fruits of repentance."

PRAYER. *Merciful Jesus, let me never forget that I will be held accountable for my decisions.*

THEREFORE, every tree that does not bear good fruit will be cut down and thrown into the fire. —Mt 3:10

JAN. 9

Beat the heat

REFLECTION. John the Baptist lived a radical life and he did not settle for anything less than what God required. His words of judgment may sound startling to our ears yet it doesn't diminish the truth of what he says.

We will be held accountable for our lives. What activities do you need to repent of and how can you be the man God calls you to be?

PRAYER. *Jesus, what You ask is difficult but with Your Holy Spirit I can accomplish Your will.*

———————————

AND a voice came from heaven, saying, "This is my beloved Son, in whom I am well pleased." —Mt 3:17

JAN. 10

Baptism seals us as sons of the Father

REFLECTION. For many of us, acquiring praise from someone we love or respect means a great deal. Encouraging words from our dad, our coaches, and our employers can mean so much.

In baptism, we too are affirmed as a beloved son of the Father even before we can respond or exhibit any faith. Such is the love of God for you.

PRAYER. *Heavenly Father, thank You for the many expressions of love for me.*

THEN Jesus was led by the Spirit into the desert to be tempted by the devil.
—Mt 4:1

JAN. 11

Are you led by the Spirit?

REFLECTION. Jesus was led by the Spirit into the desert and was tempted by the devil, so we too will experience temptations. The question becomes how will we stand against such an adversary?

When our whole lives are led by the Spirit we can resist. Who can support you when you are tempted? Who can you support?

PRAYER. *Holy Spirit, come to my aid when I am tempted and raise up good supportive friends.*

JESUS answered, "As it is written: 'Man does not live by bread alone, but by every word that comes forth from the mouth of God.'"
—Mt 4:4

JAN. 12

What's on your plate?

REFLECTION. Psychologists have developed various models declaring what gives man fulfillment and different levels of happiness. Satisfying our biological need for food, for instance, meets one criteria of happiness, but we know from experience it is not long lasting.

Jesus points us to the transcendent by calling our attention to His Word which can sustain us through any trial or hardship.

PRAYER. *Lord Jesus, let me be attentive to Your word and may I read it often.*

LOVE is therefore the fundamental and innate vocation of every human being.
—Pope Saint John Paul II, *Familiaris Consortio*

JAN.
13

Every man's true vocation

REFLECTION. The word 'vocation' has its roots in the Latin word 'vocare' which means 'to call.'

While we all try to discern what our particular call is in life and what our future will bring in both our professional and private lives, our fundamental vocation is to love. Love as defined by the person and actions of Jesus Christ is the true standard to which we are called.

PRAYER. *My Lord Jesus Christ, help me to love those who are most difficult to love.*

COME, follow me, and I will make you fishers of men.
—Mt 4:19

JAN.
14

Fishers of men or keepers of the aquarium?

REFLECTION. These words spoken by Jesus to his first disciples are familiar to most Catholics, yet I wonder if we have taken into account the cost of their discipleship? These fishermen left what was familiar to them and followed Jesus into the unknown.

Throughout history men have been attracted to the challenge of bringing others to Christ. Are you up for that challenge?

PRAYER. *Lord Jesus, here I am, use me to help bring others to You.*

E IS the reflection of God's glory and the perfect expression of his very being. —Heb 1:3

JAN. 15

Reflect Gods glory in your life

REFLECTION. Most 'die hard' sports fans are not afraid to wear their favorite team's uniform and logo with pride. From tee-shirts to hats to bumper stickers, people love to support their team and associate with them. They rejoice when they win and sulk when they lose.

As men, we are called to represent and reflect God's glory through our relationship with Christ.

PRAYER. *Holy Spirit, draw me close to Jesus so His love may be reflected in all I do.*

HEREFORE, we should pay much closer attention to what we have heard so that we do not drift away. — Heb 2:1

JAN. 16

Attention to detail

REFLECTION. Following a game plan or reading directions is vital because those instructions matter. When we follow the plan we trust that the one who wrote the instructions knows what they are doing.

In our desire to follow Jesus the details are important because God's word is the word of God.

PRAYER. *Lord Jesus, may my focus be steadfast on You and Your word at all times.*

FOR clearly he did not come to help angels but rather he came to help the descendants of Abraham.

—Heb 2:16

To protect and serve

REFLECTION. When the author of the letter to the Hebrews writes about the descendants of Abraham he is speaking about those who have the faith of Abraham.

Living a life of faith and trust in Jesus is difficult and often even our culture is against us. No need to worry however, because Jesus Himself is praying for us and offering us His assistance through the Church.

PRAYER. *My Lord and God, come to my aid and strengthen my walk of faith.*

BECAUSE he himself was tested by suffering, he is able to help those who are being tested.

—Heb 2:18

JAN. 18

Compassion and wisdom to be passed on

REFLECTION. At every age and every stage of life we learn some life lessons. Some lessons come without discomfort and some come through pain and suffering.

In the same way that Jesus offered His life to the Father, we too have opportunities to offer up our lives. How can you reach out and raise someone up who is suffering?

PRAYER. *Mother of Jesus, remind me to be like Jesus and to help those who are suffering.*

NOW Moses was faithful as a servant in God's household testifying to the things that would later be revealed.

—Heb 3:5

Be a good witness

REFLECTION. The home plays a significant role in the Bible. So much of Jesus' teaching, healing, forgiving, and sharing meals takes place not in the Temple or synagogue but in homes. We are reminded that Moses himself was "faithful" in God's household.

What would your family say about your faithfulness? Opportunities abound to live faithfully.

PRAYER. *Lord, may my faithfulness to You be lived out in my home each and every day.*

ATHER encourage each other every day.

—Heb 3:13

The value of a well-placed word

REFLECTION. Negativity seems to be everywhere these days, and because of social media people have access to the frustration of others. While there are plenty of things to complain about, the advice from St. Paul is valuable today, "encourage each other."

A well placed word of encouragement can break the cycle of negativity and let others know how valuable they are.

PRAYER. *Heavenly Father, open my eyes to those who need a word of encouragement.*

16

INDEED, the word of God is living and active.
—Heb 4:12

The power of God's word

REFLECTION. There are many great novels and various forms of literature that have been passed on down through the ages. The authors and their works are often studied throughout high school and college.

The Word of God differs because it has the power to transform us and connect us to the heart of God the Father. Take and read!

PRAYER. *Jesus, Word of God, give me a growing hunger for Your Word.*

LET us hold fast to our profession of faith
—Heb 4:14

Hold on tight, don't let go!

REFLECTION. When Catholics join together for worship we recite the Creed, a statement of what we believe. The very first line is controversial in our secular society for it reads, "I believe in God."

What a great gift indeed to proclaim that we believe in God. A God of love, mercy, and justice. Hold on to your faith, and don't deny Him who died for you.

PRAYER. *Lord God, may my faith be proclaimed by my words and in how I live my life.*

ET us then approach the throne of grace with confidence so that we may receive mercy and find grace when we are in need of help. —Heb 4:16

Know before whom you stand

REFLECTION. One of the main attributes of a successful job interview is confidence. A new suit, firm handshake, and steady eye contact all communicate confidence.

St. Paul tells us plainly to have that same confidence when we approach God with our requests. The God whom we approach is not a Wall Street executive but the God who loves us and desires the best for us.

PRAYER. *Jesus, may I never be afraid to rely on Your mercy and grace.*

MMEDIATELY, they left their boat and their father and followed him. —Mt 4:22

JAN. 24

A journey into the unknown

REFLECTION. It's not uncommon for children to leave their parents' home and start out on their own chosen path. In Jesus' day it was different. Honoring your father meant that you were under your father's authority until he died.

Following Jesus and His way calls for a radical shift from family allegiance to the Lordship of Jesus. There is a cost to following Jesus.

PRAYER. *Christ my Lord, strengthen me to follow You and not to count the cost.*

EFORE the foundation of the world he chose us in Christ to be holy and blameless in his sight and to be filled with love.

JAN. 25

—Eph 1:4

Chosen for a reason

REFLECTION. Draft day for the NFL has become more and more popular over the last twenty years. People carve out a whole day and countless hours debating in anticipation of who their team will draft. When an athlete's name is called the camera turns to them and their family and an eruption of joy ensues.

You have been called, selected, and chosen by God Himself for a great task.

PRAYER. *Jesus, my Savior, thank You for selecting me. May I be a faithful disciple.*

 N CHRIST and through his blood we have redemption and the forgiveness of our sins.

JAN. 26

—Eph 1:7

Paid in full!

REFLECTION. I was in New York City during Christmas and my car was towed. An awful experience. When I paid the outrageous fee to get my car back the receipt had written on it, "Redeemed."

I immediately thought of the reason why Christ came—for it was to redeem us. He purchased us back from death and the price was His blood.

PRAYER. *Merciful Father, thank You for redeeming me and all humanity!*

I**N HIM, you were marked with the seal of the Holy Spirit who had been promised.**
—Eph 1:13

JAN. 27

Be a bold witness

REFLECTION. The Apostles gathered together in an Upper Room as recorded in the book of Acts. Then the Holy Spirit came upon them and they were forever changed. They began to boldly proclaim the risen Lord Jesus and they were empowered to preach.

You too, have been sealed with the Holy Spirit. Tap into His power and be the man God calls you to be.

PRAYER. *Come Holy Spirit, set my heart aflame with Your love and empower me to serve Jesus.*

I**T'S better to be a child of God than the King of the whole world.**
—St. Aloysius Gonzaga

JAN. 28

Do you realize who you are?

REFLECTION. St. Aloysius Gonzaga was the son of an Italian aristocrat who became a member of the Society of Jesus (Jesuits). He died while caring for those affected by an epidemic before his twenty-fourth birthday.

One of the qualities that makes this Saint stand out is that he knew his true home was heaven. How much time do we invest thinking about heaven?

PRAYER. *Heavenly Father, make my faith and work during this life bring me to life eternal.*

E AN active presence in the community, as living cells, as living stones.

—Pope Francis

Showing up is half the battle

REFLECTION. The first community that men need to be active in is their family. The indispensable building block of humanity. The evidence is clear that children benefit greatly and prosper when a mother and father are active in their lives.

Every day is a gift and each day will present opportunities for love and care in the family. Love your children and change the world.

PRAYER. *Lord God, may my energies be focused first and foremost on my family.*

 AVING heard of your faith in the Lord Jesus and of your love towards all the saints...

—Eph 1:15

Have others heard of your faith?

REFLECTION. It's amazing all the information that we give out each day that others can pick up on. From the coffee station at work to social media, people can ascertain our political views, where we eat, and so on.

Is our faith ever a part of the conversation? Take some time to consider how you speak and act as a man of faith wherever you are.

PRAYER. *Loving Lord, may our speech and prayers be backed up by a faithful witness.*

'LL never forget that feeling I got when I heard that you got home. —Joseph Strummer

Safe at home

REFLECTION. Absence does make the heart grow fonder especially when our children and loved ones have been away. When they come for a visit there is a certain feeling that comes over us and all seems right with the world.

Heaven is described as a home, a place where we are in the company of loved ones and in the presence of God who is love.

PRAYER. *Holy Spirit, never allow me to lose sight of my true home, Heaven.*

 THEREFORE never cease to give thanks to God for you as I remember you in my prayers. —Eph 1:16

Loved and prayed for

REFLECTION. St. Paul was writing to a Christian community that had disagreements and arguments like most small groups, and his tone is that of a loving father. Rather than a sharp reprimand or condemnation he realizes that they are a young community trying to find their way in their new faith.

Who in your life do you give thanks for? Who do you remember in your prayers?

PRAYER. *Almighty God, thank You for the example of wise men you've placed in my life.*

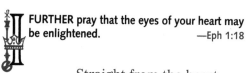 **FURTHER** pray that the eyes of your heart may be enlightened. —Eph 1:18

FEB.

2

Straight from the heart

REFLECTION. The phrase St. Paul uses to instruct the Christians who reside in Ephesus sounds a little strange, yet I think we all understand what he's saying. There are always moments in our lives when a situation just doesn't "feel" right. We can even be presented with logical facts yet something seems off.

May the eyes of our heart always be attuned to the will of God.

PRAYER. *Lord Jesus, send Your Holy Spirit to enlighten my heart, mind, and entire being.*

 UT God is rich in his mercy, and because he had such great love for us. —Eph 2:4

FEB.

3

No depth to God's mercy

REFLECTION. Often men will base their worth on what they produce or how much money they make.

Any father of a newborn child can tell you that all you have to do is simply be in the presence of the child and the love pours out of you. God's love for us is similar and it's good to acknowledge His love for us.

PRAYER. *My God, thank You for Your immeasurable love, mercy, and patience with me.*

E CANNOT be Christians part-time. If Christ is at the center of our lives, he is present in all that we do. —Pope Francis

FEB. 4

Are you all in?

REFLECTION. Every once in a while I'll find myself watching the World Series of Poker on TV. I find it interesting to watch, and there inevitably comes a point when one player will announce, I'm "all in," and he pushes all his chips to the center of the table.

In our walk with Christ we are called to go "all in" and hold nothing back.

PRAYER. *Jesus, I am "all in" for You as You are "all in" for me.*

 HE most deadly poison of our time is indifference. —St. Maximillian Kolbe

FEB. 5

Little things do matter

REFLECTION. St. Maximillian Kolbe was a Catholic priest who voluntarily gave his life so another man could live. This occurred during the Holocaust at Auschwitz.

This saint is not a saint for how he died but for how he lived. This last sacrifice was only one in a long series of actions in which he put others first. Love always wins in the end.

PRAYER. *Loving God, send Your Spirit to stir within me to be a man of action.*

FOR we are God's handiwork. —Eph 2:10 **FEB.**

6

Designed for a great purpose

REFLECTION. How many times have we said upon meeting the son of a friend something along the lines of, "you have your father's eyes; you have your dad's smile." We do replicate ourselves in our children not only with physical characteristics but in mannerisms.

God is not embodied, but throughout scripture it's clear that we are His handiwork, created in His image and likeness.

PRAYER. *Jesus, may others see Your presence in me and may I appreciate the gift of life.*

LESSED is the man who does not walk in the counsel of the wicked. —Ps 1:1 **FEB.**

7

Choose your counselors carefully

REFLECTION. The phrase "walk in" has special significance throughout the scriptures. It's difficult to circumvent all evil and to avoid those with evil schemes. What the author of the Psalms is warning us about is seeking advice from those who are intentional in their deceit.

Thank God for His wisdom and for those who have advised you with their wisdom.

PRAYER. *Lord, may Your blessing be upon me, and may Your hand guide my steps.*

ATHER, his delight is in the law of the Lord, and on that law he meditates day and night. —Ps 1:2

FEB. 8

Think about it

REFLECTION. The man of God "meditates" on God's law day and night. This is something that most men have not witnessed in other men so it seems strange to us.

Yet the truth of the matter is clear, when God's law becomes part of us we tend to act in a way consistent with His word. May His Word guide our thoughts and all of our actions.

PRAYER. *Lord, may meditating on Your Word be my "new normal."*

 OR the Lord watches over the way of the righteous. —Ps 1:6

FEB. 9

Ever watchful, ever faithful

REFLECTION. God loves all His children, both the faithful and the faithless. Yet the Psalmist is clear that the person who disregards God's Word will perish.

His word is a light to our path and a guide to living a meaningful life. What does it mean for you to be virtuous, honorable, and righteous?

PRAYER. *Lord God, watch over my steps and increase my desire to serve You.*

DO CHOOSE, be made clean. —Mt 8:3 **FEB.**
10

The response is yes!

REFLECTION. Jesus is approached by a man with leprosy, a dreaded skin disease, who asked that he be made clean. Jesus' response is clear and he heals him. The leprosy vanished and the man had a chance at a new life.

In what area of your life do you need to be healed? Approach Jesus with the leper's confidence and you can experience God's loving touch as well.

PRAYER. *Lord Jesus, grant me the courage to face the areas where I need healing.*

IN NO one throughout Israel have I found faith as great as this. —Mt 8:10 **FEB.**
11

Where is your faith?

REFLECTION. Jesus highlights the faith of a Roman centurion who asked for help for his servant. His response is familiar to Catholics for we repeat it during Mass. "Lord, I am not worthy that you should come under my roof. But simply say the word and my soul will be healed."

When have you exhibited this type of faith?

PRAYER. *Lord, I do believe but help my faith to be as strong as the centurion's faith.*

E TOUCHED her hand and the fever left her, and she got up and began to serve him. —Mt 8:15

FEB.
12

Receive and then give

REFLECTION. The miracle of the healing of Peter's mother-in-law is recorded in three Gospels yet neither Jesus nor the woman say a word. He heals with a touch and she responds with service. They both are without words but not without witness.

How can you lift others up with both your actions and words? How can you serve Jesus through serving others?

PRAYER. *My God, help me to be a man of both healing words and actions.*

 HY are you so frightened, O you of little faith? —Mt 8:26

FEB.
13

Who are you going with?

REFLECTION. "O you of little faith" is a phrase that Jesus repeats five times to His Apostles in Matthew's Gospel. We forget that these men were also on a journey of faith and discovering for themselves just who Jesus was.

They would discover, as do we, that Jesus is trustworthy, He is God. No need to fear; He is with us.

PRAYER. *Jesus, distill my fear and comfort me with the truth that You are ever near.*

TAKE heart, son. Your sins are forgiven.
—Mt 9:2

FEB.
14

Forgiveness before healing

REFLECTION. Jesus heals and restores a man who was brought to him by four friends. These four friends overcame obstacles, collaborated, and were persistent in their desire to get to Jesus. Before Jesus healed the man He first forgave his sins.

Many people desire a healing but few take the time to forgive. Who might God be calling you to forgive?

PRAYER. *Lord Jesus, may I forgive as freely as You forgive.*

WHY do you harbor evil thoughts in your hearts?
—Mt 9:4

FEB.
15

Have versus harbor

REFLECTION. It's not uncommon to have evil thoughts. Someone cuts you off in traffic, cuts in line ahead of you, and more serious offenses can prompt evil thoughts. Jesus warns against harboring them which is different.

What do you allow space in your heart for? Ask for the grace to let go of evil thoughts and be filled with the Holy Spirit.

PRAYER. *God of Mercy, assist me in letting go of evil thoughts.*

FOLLOW me, and he got up and followed him. —Mt 9:9

FEB.
16

Radical commitment

REFLECTION. The call of Matthew the tax collector by Jesus is dramatic and the response is resolute. In that brief encounter Matthew's life forever changes.

His "yes" to Jesus set his life in a direction that continues to impact the world through his discipleship and writing. While no "yes" is recorded in his words, his actions speak loud and clear.

PRAYER. *Jesus, may my actions show of my discipleship, my following You.*

WHEN he was sitting at dinner in the house... —Mt 9:10

FEB.
17

Significant meals

REFLECTION. How many meals have you eaten thus far in your life? I can't even imagine what that number may be, but no doubt it's in the thousands. Meals are still important for we share not only food but our very lives as well.

Think of the most significant meal you've ever eaten. Most likely it was significant for who was there. Your presence is valuable to your family.

PRAYER. *My Lord, You are present at each Mass, thank You for Your Eucharistic presence.*

T IS not the healthy who need a physician, but rather those who are sick. —Mt 9:12

FEB.
18

An eye for the poor

REFLECTION. Jesus was certainly a man for others. He used His miraculous powers for people when they were sick, infirm, and hungry.

As followers of Jesus you have been given some gifts which should be used to assist others regardless of what they believe. Perhaps in serving others they may glimpse God's presence in you.

PRAYER. *Come Holy Spirit, use me to serve Jesus in others.*

 LESSED are all those who take refuge in him. —Ps 2:12

FEB.
19

"Gimmie" shelter

REFLECTION. In the biblical world of the Old Testament what people were looking for shelter from ranged from the rule of foreign enemies to the midday heat.

We are not much different in seeking safety and protection from the elements and people who may do us harm. Like them, we do well to turn to the Lord who is there to save us.

PRAYER. *Father Almighty, save me from harm and may I bring others to You.*

ISTEN to my words, O Lord; pay heed to my sighs.
—Ps 5:2

FEB.
20

Faith faces reality

REFLECTION. It's a misconception to think "religious" people are immune from pain and suffering. Jesus endured both and King David, the author of the Psalms, is in a deep state of despair as he writes.

The lesson for us is to follow the example of Jesus and King David and let the pain in our heart rise to the throne of God.

PRAYER. *Jesus, Mary, and Joseph, listen to my words and strengthen me for the journey.*

LORD, our Lord, how glorious is your name in all the earth!
—Ps 8:10

FEB.
21

What's in a name?

REFLECTION. Many sports stars are known by just their last name. Ruth, Jordan, Gretzky, and Lombardi come immediately to mind. Their names recall their greatness and achievements while they were in the game.

Of all the names ever spoken, only one has power to heal and redeem. Our Lord and God is glorious and His name recalls His greatness.

PRAYER. *My Lord, my God, may Your name always be mentioned with honor and praise.*

UT you note our troubles and our grief so that you may resolve our difficulties.
—Ps 10:14

FEB.
22

Unspoken but not unhidden

REFLECTION. There are often times when men hide their sorrow and troubles. After all, being strong and silent is part of what makes a man in our culture. While we may bury troubles deep within God knows what's going on and He takes note.

A healthy prayer life includes casting our cares on Him for He cares for you. Share your burden with Him.

PRAYER. *Merciful Jesus, examine my heart, resolve my difficulties.*

ELP, O Lord, for there are no godly left.
—Ps 12:2

FEB.
23

Doesn't anyone else believe?

REFLECTION. Being faithful to Christ and His Church is rewarding yet difficult. Our culture has taken God out of the marketplace and to admit you are a faithful Catholic places you in the minority.

Fear not, you are not alone for there are others who still believe and are even being persecuted for the faith. God sees your faith and believes in you.

PRAYER. *Almighty God, surround me with other men who believe.*

HE fool says in his heart, "There is no God." —Ps 14:1

FEB. 24

What a fool believes

REFLECTION. The Bible is very straightforward when it comes to those who are righteous and to those who are not. The word fool appears around 120 times in the scriptures and most often refers to those who are not righteous and have a disregard for wisdom and instruction.

God is our hope, He is present even when He may be silent.

PRAYER. *Lord Jesus, never let me despair to the point of unbelief.*

 KEEP the Lord always before me. —Ps 16:8

FEB. 25

Always on my mind

REFLECTION. The long distance runner experiences ups and downs along the course. The runners "high" is only experienced after many miles of running and many hours of training.

What helps the runner continue when every fiber in his body cries out to stop? It's the finish line! Keep your eyes fixed on the finish line, and that will focus your heart and mind.

PRAYER. *Jesus, may You be my focus from sun up to sun down.*

Y STEPS have held fast to your paths; my feet have not wavered.

FEB.
26

—Ps 17:5

Every step you take

REFLECTION. Living in a region of the country where it snows can be a nuisance and present opportunities for great fun. To follow in the big footprints of someone who walks ahead of you in the snow makes walking easier.

As a man, who will follow in your "footsteps"? Will you hold fast to the path that God's Word has set before you?

PRAYER. *God of Light, illuminate my way to see clearly my path in life.*

HE precepts of the Lord are right, causing the heart to rejoice.

FEB.
27

—Ps 19:9

Rejoicing inside out

REFLECTION. When things are just right there is something inside us that just "clicks." We may not even have the words to describe it, but when our mind accepts an idea and our heart is drawn to it, we seem to have a purpose which fulfills us.

Following the precepts of the Lord does cause our heart to rejoice because God wills only the best for us.

PRAYER. *Lord, You are the reason I rejoice each day; guide my steps!*

N ADULT faith does not follow the
waves of fashion and the latest novelties. —Pope Benedict XVI

**FEB.
28**

True, tried, and tested

REFLECTION. How many times have we heard
people born in certain eras described as millen-
nials, Generation X, Generation Y, children of
the '60s and so on?

While these descriptions may call to mind
fashion, music, and technology trends, those
who follow Christ follow Him alone. The truths
of our faith remain firm as does our trust in
Jesus.

PRAYER. *Lord, may my focus be on You. Mold
me into the man You desire me to be.*

 HERE'S more inside you that you
haven't shown. —Paul Weller

**FEB.
29**

When we're in a jam

REFLECTION. It's been said that immense pressure can turn coal either into a diamond or to
dust. The same can be said of men. Pressure can
humble us to despair or we can become stronger
after being tested.

When the pressure seems too much to handle,
Christians learn that we have great recourse in
the Holy Spirit who empowers us for God's will.

PRAYER. *Holy Spirit, empower me to be the
man who stands up for You and others.*

JUDE, a servant of Jesus Christ.

—Jude 1

**MAR.
1**

Who do you serve?

REFLECTION. Imagine being one of the twelve Apostles or one of the people that Jesus healed in scripture. I would think that there would be cause for some boasting because after all, they knew Jesus, were touched by Him.

However, when writing letters, these men who encountered Jesus refer to themselves as servants of Jesus. Are we any less servants of Christ?

PRAYER. *Jesus my Savior, let me remember that it is You whom I serve in this life.*

HOLINESS is not an aim; it is a result. The aim of union is to please God.

—Mother Celine Borzęcka

**MAR.
2**

Our aim is true

REFLECTION. If holiness was easy everyone would be a saint. The good news is that we are not alone in our efforts to be the man of God He calls us to be.

It begins with the desire to please God in all areas of our life. When this is our aim and with the help of the Holy Spirt, we are on the road to holiness.

PRAYER. *Jesus, may my aim be true in pleasing You today and every day!*

T IS these people who create divisions, who **MAR.** follow their natural instincts and do not possess the Spirit. —Jude 19 **3**

United, not divided

REFLECTION. Throughout the New Testament we find the authors writing to the Christian communities warning them about those who cause divisions. Like any sports team or business, the seeds of division break down the team.

As Catholics we are called to seek unity, to bring people together. How can you be part of the solution even in your own family?

PRAYER. *Holy Trinity, may our family be united in love and help bring peace to others.*

AVE compassion for those who are **MAR.** wavering. —Jude 22 **4**

Men of valor and honor

REFLECTION. We all desire to hear the words, "Well done, my good and faithful servant," at the end of our days. One image that challenges me is that while standing at the "pearly gates," I hear the question, "Who have you brought with you?"

St. Jude reminds us to have compassion and to help those who are wavering. Who may that be in your life?

PRAYER. *Mary, Queen of Heaven, pray for me that I may help those who are wavering.*

AND this is love: when we walk according to his commandments.

—2 Jn 6

Walk this way

REFLECTION. How many times do we associate love with a feeling or emotion? Certainly there are times when our emotions and passions flood our hearts but we know from experience that those feelings fade.

The Apostle John makes the connection between love and obedience to God's Word. Where is the face of love? In those who follow His commandments day by day.

PRAYER. *Lord, may I be faithful in following Your commandments.*

———————

PLEASE continue to help them on their journey in a manner worthy of God.

—3 Jn 6

The method and the manner

REFLECTION. Often it's how we say something and not what we say that people take offense at. Perhaps we are tired or angry and the message we intend to communicate is lost.

In serving God, the manner in which we assist and serve does matter. We love because He loved us first. May we always aim to serve God and others in an honorable manner.

PRAYER. *Jesus, may I see Your face in all those whom I serve and speak to this day.*

ELOVED, do not imitate what is evil; rather, imitate what is good. —3 Jn 11

Imitate and replicate the good

REFLECTION. My wife and I witness on a daily basis how our four children can imitate what they see on TV and even imitate us. It's usually a funny TV show they re-enact or a certain voice inflection my wife and I use, and they are spot on in their impersonation.

It reminds us that our actions and words do get noticed and we replicate ourselves in our children.

PRAYER. *Lord, may my example be a good witness to my family and to other men.*

HERE was a blameless and upright man named Job, who feared God and avoided evil. —Job 1:1

How are you known?

REFLECTION. Our culture seems to reinforce the importance of how much money we make, our professional titles, and what side of the political fence we cast our lot with. Not so with the Bible.

The standard for the man of God is really quite simple, and we see it in the description of Job. Blameless and upright, he feared God and avoided evil.

PRAYER. *Jesus, forgive me for those times I was not the man You made me to be.*

HE Lord gave and the Lord has taken away; blessed be the name of the Lord.
—Job 1:21

9

The patience of Job

REFLECTION. When we put God first in our lives we can rest assure that He is in charge in every area of our life. Job was such a man who knew that every good gift he received came from God.

He also realized that God allows bad things to happen to good people for a purpose that He alone knows. Job indeed had patience and he also learned to trust.

PRAYER. *Lord God, may I bless Your name in all the circumstances of my life.*

 HAT is man, that you make much of him, or pay him any heed?
—Job 7:17

MAR.

10

Who are we in God's sight?

REFLECTION. Job was a man who knew personal suffering. His children were killed and his body bore the brunt of disease.

We, like Job, at times may be tempted to ask who are we in God's sight? Job saw partially, but we who believe in God see fully that we are worth the life of His Son, Jesus Christ. Yes, God loves you immensely.

PRAYER. *Thank You God, for showing Your love to all through the life of Your Son.*

41

FROM the commands of his lips I have not departed; the words of his mouth I have treasured in my heart. —Job 23:12

Unpredictable but not unfaithful

REFLECTION. It just seems unfair at times. We follow the rules, we say our prayers and still life does not go as we planned. God, "Where are you?" Job has the same dilemma that we experience when we are in the midst of a storm.

This is where our faith kicks in, where the "rubber meets the road." Can we still be faithful when things don't go as we planned?

PRAYER. *St. Joseph, hear my cry for help, may I never lose my faith despite my confusion.*

GIRD up your loins now, like a man; I will question you, and you tell me the answers! —Job 38:3

The voice of God

REFLECTION. God speaks to Job after Job and his friends discuss the question of suffering. While we might expect a soft and gentle reply from God what we get is just the opposite. God bombards Job with a series of questions.

These questions are difficult but they have a purpose. They remind Job that God is God and he is not and what is needed is trust.

PRAYER. *My God, I know You love me, let me hear Your voice in the midst of the storm.*

I HAD heard of you by word of mouth, but now my eye has seen you. —Job 42:5

The importance of encounter

REFLECTION. Too often people who attend religious education classes or Catholic schools go through a program but never encounter the person of Jesus Christ.

It's the encounter with the living God that makes all the difference. Without that encounter religion seems like a list of rules and regulations devoid of meaning. Can you articulate your encounter with God?

PRAYER. *Jesus, give me the confidence to speak of my encounter with You to other men.*

THAT men may appreciate wisdom and discipline, may understand words of intelligence. —Prov 1:2

Wisdom from above

REFLECTION. The author of the book of Proverbs has left a great gift to humankind because his writing gives very practical advice which is applicable today. It is a roadmap to dealing with various people, situations, and even God.

Imagine being lost in a foreign country with no map. The Proverbs are instructions for daily living so we don't lose our way.

PRAYER. *Heavenly Father, may Your Word guide my steps as I am attuned to Your will.*

THE fear of the Lord is the beginning of wisdom.

—Prov 1:7

MAR.
15

Peace comes with order

REFLECTION. It was St. Augustine who said, "Peace is the tranquility of order."When things are in order in our lives we do have a certain peace. Not everything is in our control, but we can control certain aspects of our lives.

Having God in His rightful place is the first step in having order in our lives. Peace follows. Without having God first, chaos is sure to follow.

PRAYER. *Jesus, may I give You first priority of my day that I may handle whatever life has in store.*

TRUST in the Lord with all your heart, on your own intelligence rely not.

—Prov 3:5

MAR.
16

In all of your ways

REFLECTION. God has given man a mind so that he can reason. In fact, many people come to a belief in God through reasoning and asking the big questions such as why we are here.

However, when it comes to reason we also know that our mind is finite, we can't know it all. We need to trust God in all things.

PRAYER. *Jesus, my Good Shepherd, guide me by Your Word and Spirit.*

UT away from you dishonest talk, deceitful speech put far from you. —Prov 4:24

Be a man of your word

REFLECTION. There was a time when a man's word was his bond. Now it seems contracts and lawyers are involved in almost every agreement we make. Perhaps there are good reasons for that due to dishonest and deceitful people.

As a man of God truthfulness should be something we are known for. Decide today that your speech will be honest and forthright.

PRAYER. *Lord, forgive me for those times I have been deceitful in word and deed.*

 ATRED stirs up disputes, but love covers all offenses. —Prov 10:12

Choose love each day

REFLECTION. The author of the book of Proverbs likes to contrast wisdom with folly, poverty with riches, and vice with virtue. Here he speaks of hatred and love.

How true that when we are confronted with hatred our immediate reaction may be to return the hate and extend the divide between the other. Love, on the other hand, seems to heal all wounds.

PRAYER. *Jesus, You showed only love to those who hurt You; may I do no less.*

HEN pride comes, disgrace comes; but with the humble is wisdom.

MAR.
19

—Prov 11:2

Humility through humiliation at times

REFLECTION. Being humiliated is a very painful event. It matters not if it occurs on the ball field, the classroom, or a courtroom; no one likes to be humiliated.

It's true that "pride goes before the fall" but what lessons can we learn from the experience. We can be humble and thank God for the gifts we have, and we can point to God as the source of all goodness.

PRAYER. *Jesus, teach me wisdom and humility in all my actions and thoughts.*

 HE will of God guides us and knows better what is good for us.

MAR.
20

—Mother Celine Borzęcka

Ever faithful to the will of God

REFLECTION. Mother Borzęcka was the foundress of the Sisters of the Resurrection. She desired the religious life but married in obedience to her parents and bore four children. After her husband's death, she chose to follow the spiritual path with her daughter at her side.

God always has a plan and His will is accomplished in His time.

PRAYER. *Jesus, help me to support those who are discerning a call to religious life.*

O MOMENT can be wasted, no opportunity missed, since each has a purpose in man's life, each has a purpose in God's plan. —Fr. Walter J. Ciszek, S.J.

Each day is a gift

REFLECTION. Fr. Ciszek has one of the most fascinating stories of the twentieth century. As a priest he was exiled north of the Arctic Circle by the Soviets where he endured years of hard labor.

In his book, *He Leadeth Me*, he speaks of his ordeal all the while seeing the hand of God in his life. As you move forward in life make the most of each opportunity as Fr. Ciszek did.

PRAYER. *Merciful Jesus, help me to make the most of each day and to see trials as opportunities.*

 HE way of the fool seems right in his own eyes, but he who listens to advice is wise. —Prov 12:15

Good counsel is priceless

REFLECTION. No one likes to be a fool and there is only so much we can know. The Proverbs speak of seeking good counsel which is sound advice today.

We don't need to know it all so it's a good practice to cultivate the thoughts and opinions of trustworthy, faithful friends to help us along the way. When asked, share your wisdom as well.

PRAYER. *Lord, what You ask calls for humility, raise up for me wise friends.*

MILD answer calms wrath, but a **MAR.** harsh word stirs up anger. —Prov 15:1

23

Think before you speak

REFLECTION. How many times do we wish we could go back in time to take back the words that just came out of our mouth? These moments usually occur when we are angry and in the heat of an argument.

The next time a harsh word is spoken to you take the high road and respond with a mild answer. You may surprise yourself and the other person!

PRAYER. *Blessed Mother, may the words of my mouth be respectful and mild.*

 HE mind of the intelligent man seeks **MAR.** knowledge. —Prov 15:14

24

Never stop learning

REFLECTION. Our formal education may cease in our early twenties, but we should never lose our thirst for knowledge. Hobbies and sports can keep the body in shape and the mind active so these are good things to pursue.

We should also be challenged to grow in our faith. The *Catechism of the Catholic Church*, the lives of the Saints, and other aspects of theology and philosophy are waiting for you.

PRAYER. *Jesus, increase my hunger for wisdom and knowledge about the faith.*

LANS fail when there is no counsel, but succeed when counselors are many.

—Prov 15:22

Don't go it alone

REFLECTION. Hollywood has made a fortune over the years portraying Super Heroes as the strong silent type. It even goes back to the 1940s and '50s with the iconic Cowboy who rides the range alone.

Reality is not like that, and the advice in Proverbs can give us pause to think if we utilize the wisdom of our family, friends, and community when we execute a plan.

PRAYER. *Gracious Father, teach me to rely on the wisdom of faithful people whom I trust.*

 OMETIMES a way seems right to a man, but the end of it leads to death.

—Prov 16:25

We may not be our own best counsel

REFLECTION. We have all experienced times when we absolutely, 100% believed we were in the right only to find out that we weren't. We just didn't take into account unforeseen circumstances and things that were out of our control.

There are few things in life we can be 100% sure of except that God loves us through it all.

PRAYER. *Lord, I try my best to please You. Bless my actions so they don't end in death.*

GOOD name is more desirable than great riches, and high esteem, than gold or silver. —Prov 22:1

A name you can trust

REFLECTION. Advertisers spend millions of dollars on branding their products and placing them in the best light. When a scandal occurs harming the product or the company name panic sets in.

God's Word is clear when it comes to our good name and the value it has. Even if we are falsely accused, may our virtue and good name be a shield from the storm.

PRAYER. *Lord God, may my conduct be reflective of Your hand on my life.*

 O SHOW partiality in judgment is not good. —Prov 24:23

The golden median

REFLECTION. There have been times in my life when I have literally yelled at my TV set when watching a NY Rangers hockey game. Obviously the officials were paid off by the other team or so it seems.

This gives me pause to think about my own judgments and how fair and just I am when it comes to making decisions.

PRAYER. *Jesus, just judge that You are, may my judgments be based on truth and justice.*

DO NOT answer fools according to their folly, lest you too become like them.

—Prov 26:4

Hold your tongue, don't hit send!

REFLECTION. It can be so tempting to respond to a foolish remark with a quick retort. It's even more tempting on social media or through email to respond in a way which is clever since the person is not in front of us.

The wisdom in this proverb is clear and useful today. Better to just let it go and turn the page as they say.

PRAYER. *Lord God, forgive me those times I engaged in foolish conversations.*

AS DOGS return to their vomit, so fools repeat their folly. —Prov 26:11

MAR.
30

Don't make the same mistake twice

REFLECTION. Doing something foolish is different than being a fool. Part of the human experience consists of a series of mistakes, successes, failures, and triumphs.

The advice in Proverbs uses a powerful image to warn those who are wise to learn from their mistakes. Accept God's forgiveness for mistakes made and learn from that mistake as you move forward.

PRAYER. *Lord, grant me wisdom and prudence as I follow Your example.*

T'S the aim of existence to offer resistance to the flow of time. —Peter Shelley

MAR. 31

Finding our way home

REFLECTION. There is something in the human spirit that desires adventure and men have set out to new and distant lands throughout history seeking the unknown.

We speak in terms of chronological time, and chronologically God dwells in a different dimension—the spirit realm—beyond the perception of our physical senses. God entered into our time and thus made it holy.

PRAYER. *Holy Lord, thank You for the incarnation, for entering into the world as one of us.*

 HAVE baptized you with water, but he will baptize you with the Holy Spirit. —Mk 1:8

APR. 1

Water and Spirit

REFLECTION. John the Baptist had a singular mission: to prepare the way for Jesus the Christ. He recognized his role and executed it with precision. While Jesus is the Word of God, John the Baptist is the voice, the one who prepares the way.

As men of God, we are called to lead others to Christ through our words and actions. Have you led anyone to Jesus?

PRAYER. *St. John the Baptist, may I lead others to Jesus as you did.*

Y OU are my beloved Son; in you I am
well pleased.
—Mk 1:11

APR.
2

Father, Son and Holy Spirit

REFLECTION. There is a bond between a Father
and all his children be they boys or girls. While
God is Spirit and without gender the terminology
of the scriptures speaks of the Fatherhood of God.

Fathers and mothers are complimentary in
their roles and therefore reflect God in their
unity. What a gift for both men and women to
model the love of God.

PRAYER. *Jesus, You were loved for who You are
and not for what You did; help me accept that
love.*

I MMEDIATELY, they abandoned their nets
and followed him
—Mk 1:18

APR.
3

For a greater glory

REFLECTION. The question we often ask ourselves
when making decisions is: "What will this cost
me?" Will it cost me money, time, commitment?

When Jesus called these men they didn't
count the cost. They gave up what they couldn't
keep to gain what they couldn't lose...eternal
life. When following Christ remember no one
outdoes God in generosity.

PRAYER. *Praise You Jesus, may I never look
back in my desire to follow You.*

53

E SILENT, and come out of him.
—Mk 1:25

4

Exorcised

REFLECTION. Satan is real. There are evil spirits. These two statements may sound a bit old fashioned today and many think that every modern ill can be treated through psychology and medicine.

Jesus regularly confronted and spoke about evil spirits so the sceptic should look again. Jesus has power over all which includes Satan and evil spirits.

PRAYER. *St. Michael, defend me when I am being spiritually attacked.*

ESUS approached her, grasped her by the hand, and helped her up. —Mk 1:31

APR.
5

Without a word

REFLECTION. I find it remarkable that the early Christians recorded this miracle. No words escape the lips of either Jesus or the nameless mother-in-law; yet a miracle occurs.

How, like Jesus, can you take the initiative in reaching out and lifting up others through your actions? Without a word you can impact another's life and lift them up.

PRAYER. *Loving Lord, open my eyes to see who might need to be "lifted up" and cared for.*

ARLY the next morning, long before dawn, he arose and went off to a secluded place, where he prayed. —Mk 1:35

Make time for prayer

REFLECTION. One way to discover what priorities a person has in their life is to look at where they spend their time. If working out is important to them they will make time for that activity and "hit the gym" on a regular basis.

Jesus made prayer a priority. Is prayer a priority in your life? How can you schedule time for prayer each day?

PRAYER. *Jesus, help me to become a man of prayer.*

ON, your sins are forgiven. —Mk 2:5

Forgiveness before healing

REFLECTION. Jesus forgives a paralyzed man who was carried by four friends. After they lowered the man through the roof Jesus looks up, sees their faith, and then forgives the man. Only after Jesus forgives him does He heal the man.

How often do we desire the healing but not the work of forgiveness? Perhaps, as men of God, forgiving others is the miracle.

PRAYER. *Merciful Jesus, may I be as forgiving as You are.*

JESUS said to him, "Follow me," and he got up and followed him. —Mk 2:14

APR.
8

No going back

REFLECTION. Sometimes people think that they will follow God in their own time, when it's convenient. Matthew the tax collector is an example of a man without a "Plan B" who immediately accepts Jesus' invitation to follow Him.

Is Jesus your steering wheel or your spare tire? Discipleship has a cost and a reward. Disciples of Jesus don't count the cost.

PRAYER. *St. Matthew, pray for me that I may give my all as you did.*

WHY does he eat with tax collectors and sinners? —Mk 2:16

APR.
9

Sharing meals, sharing life

REFLECTION. Why did Jesus eat with tax collectors and sinners? Not a bad question from the religious establishment in Jesus' day. Yet Jesus' actions reveal the heart of God, the God of love and mercy who always has an eye for those on the margins.

Who can you reach out to, lend a hand, or share a meal with? This is the work of God.

PRAYER. *Lord Jesus, may I have an eye for those on the margins as You do.*

HAVE come to call not the righteous but sinners. —Mk 2:17

APR. 10

We are all sinners

REFLECTION. The word for sin is made up of three small letters. Yet at the heart of sin and in the middle of the word is that little letter "i."

Putting "I" at the center of our lives instead of God leads to a life of selfishness where we never can experience the joy that God desires for each one of us. Who is at the center of your life?

PRAYER. *Jesus, root out of me all sin and self-ishness so that You may be Lord of my life.*

 O YOU, O Lord, I lift up my soul; in you, O my God, I trust. —Ps 25:1

APR. 11

Men who give all

REFLECTION. There is a story concerning Moses when he raised his hands to part the Red Sea. The story records that the sea did not part until one man walked forward into the water.

He walked up to his knees, then his waist, then his chest, and it was only when the water reached his neck did the waters part. We walk in faith and trust.

PRAYER. *Lord, help me not to miss opportunities to trust in You.*

ND whenever unclean spirits saw him, they would fall at his feet and shout, "You are the Son of God". —Mk 3:11

Even demons acknowledge Jesus is God

REFLECTION. We pray during the Our Father: "lead us not into temptation." The holiness of Jesus caused demons to flee instead of trying to tempt Him.

As a man of God, we too, will be tempted, but imagine being so holy that demons flee from us. Living under the Lordship of Jesus is a way of life, something that demons fail to do.

PRAYER. *Mary, Mother of God, pray for me to be as bold as your Son, Jesus.*

 ESUS then went up onto the mountain and summoned those whom he wanted. —Mk 3:13

Selected and chosen

REFLECTION. In accomplishing the Father's Will on Earth Jesus did have a plan. His plan was evangelization and His method was men. No doubt Jesus prayed and discerned what men He would choose to carry His message to the rest of the world.

You have been chosen by your baptism to continue this mission of bringing others to Christ strengthened by the sacraments.

PRAYER. *Jesus, here I am, use me this day to share Your message.*

HOEVER does the will of God is my brother and sister and mother.
—Mk 3:35

APR. 14

Family redefined

REFLECTION. In the Middle East, generations of genealogy and history are memorized by family members and can be recited on demand. Jesus was well aware of this and wanted to make a point of defining who family members are in the Kingdom of God.

Quite simply, it's those who do the will of God. What opportunities to do God's will await you?

PRAYER. *Our Father, thank You for the family invitation, may I always strive to do Your will.*

———

N ANOTHER occasion he began to teach by the side of the lake.
—Mk 4:1

APR. 15

Anytime, anywhere

REFLECTION. Formal education usually takes place in a classroom, but we all know that instruction and learning can take place anywhere. Some of the most valuable lessons men learn are from their fathers, grandfathers, and uncles along the way.

Jesus was known primarily as a teacher, and He can still instruct through His word and Spirit anytime and anywhere. Are you His student?

PRAYER. *Jesus, school me in the lessons You want me to know and to pass on to others.*

A S HE sowed, some seed fell on the path. —Mk 4:4

Never forced

REFLECTION. Sharing the Good News of Jesus is a requirement of all disciples. The desire to share is an act of the Holy Spirit, yet the method some people use is most certainly not.

In this parable of the sower and the seed the seed is never forced into the ground. It must be received by the soil and by the receptive heart which is ready to accept God's Word.

PRAYER. *Lord Jesus, prepare my heart to receive Your Word in all seasons, at all times.*

H E EXPLAINED everything to his disciples when they were by themselves. —Mk 4:34

Jesus was patient with His disciples

REFLECTION. We see glimpses throughout the Gospel when Jesus takes the disciples away to pray together or to explain certain things to them. What a blessed time that must have been and how they must have treasured that time.

Who are the people in your life who have given you the gift of their time? How can you mentor others and share your knowledge of a subject?

PRAYER. *Jesus my teacher, remind me to give back to others who are struggling along the way.*

LET us cross over to the other side.

—Mk 4:35

Where is your "other side"?

REFLECTION. The four Gospels mention approximately 27 small Jewish villages outside of Jerusalem. Jesus and His disciples were comfortable in these towns because of the shared customs and religious practices.

The "other side" was the non-Jewish side. Traveling outside of their comfort zone was something Jesus was suggesting to them.

PRAYER. *Lord Jesus, may I follow where You lead even if it's outside my comfort zone.*

QUIET! Be still!

—Mk 4:39

Was Jesus only commanding the storm?

REFLECTION. In one of the most dramatic scenes in the Gospels Jesus stands up in the midst of a storm on the sea and commands: "Quiet, be still." While the storm died down I wonder if the storm inside of the disciples calmed down as well.

Allow the words of Jesus, "Peace! Be still," to stand guard over your heart and mind in every situation.

PRAYER. *Jesus, Lord and Master, calm my fear and remind me that I need to be still and quiet each day.*

HY are you so frightened? Are you still without faith? —Mk 4:40

Help my faith Lord!

REFLECTION. Perhaps we should not be so hard on ourselves for our lack of faith because we see Jesus challenging His disciples with this question many times throughout the Gospels.

The fact is that we can succumb to fear and our faith can be shaken. In those times when we are weak we need to humbly ask God our Father for the gift of faith.

PRAYER. *St. Peter, pray for us who are still on the journey that we may be men of faith.*

HEN he asked him, "What is your name?" —Mk 5:9

Relationship, relationship, relationship

REFLECTION. In one of the most bizarre scenes in the Gospels Jesus is confronted by a man possessed by an unclean spirit who harms himself and who lives in the tombs. Jesus begins with a question;"What is your name?"

We, too, may come across some unusual people and situations, but with Jesus we can approach them unafraid of the unknown.

PRAYER. *Lord Jesus, may I see the humanity in others and recognize Your handiwork in them.*

GO HOME to your own people and tell them what the Lord has done for you, and how he has had mercy on you.

APR.
22

—Mk 5:19

A missionary heart at home

REFLECTION. The Church has a vast history of men who were sent to faraway lands to spread the Good News at risk of their own lives. These men faced different languages, cultures, and diseases in order to communicate the Gospel of Jesus Christ.

Before we head out to foreign lands maybe we should reflect on how we have communicated God's love to those in our own home.

PRAYER. *Thank You Lord for Your mercy! I will share that mercy with those in my family.*

DO NOT be afraid. Just have faith.

APR.
23

—Mk 5:36

The remedy for doubt

REFLECTION. One cannot go to the store or order "faith" through the internet. Yet, Jesus says clearly, "Just have faith."

Faith is obviously more than an intellectual assent to certain truths we believe and involves action. Our faith is not in the unknown but in the person of Jesus who is with us every step of the way.

PRAYER. *Come Holy Spirit, increase my faith in Jesus and in His Word.*

IS THIS not the carpenter, the son of Mary?
—Mk 6:3

More than a carpenter

REFLECTION. Jesus faces rejection by His own townspeople early on in His public ministry. In fact, we are told that Jesus is amazed at their lack of faith.

People will have various reactions to Jesus and outright rejection is sure to be one of them. As a man of faith you are called to be a light to the world, an example for others to follow.

PRAYER. *Jesus, may my life be a reflection of Your life in the world.*

CALLING the twelve together, he began to send them out two by two.
—Mk 6:7

Made for mission

REFLECTION. Jesus will send the twelve out into the world after His resurrection in what is called the Great Commission. Here however, Jesus gives them a taste of mission, sending them out two by two.

Have you ever thought of yourself as a missionary? Every Catholic man has, by virtue of their baptism, a mission to bring the light of Christ everywhere they go.

PRAYER. *Heavenly Father, equip me for those "mission moments" that avail themselves to me every day.*

GO EASY, step lightly, stay free.
—Mick Jones

**APR.
26**

A clash of values

REFLECTION. A value is something important and evident in our lives. We may think good health is of great value, but if there is no evidence of a healthy lifestyle we deceive ourselves.

A life of faith requires first and foremost an adherence to the person of Jesus Christ. When there is evidence that Jesus is at the center of our lives, we can be free.

PRAYER. *My Lord and my all, direct my steps to the beat of Your Sacred Heart.*

———————

HEROD was afraid of John, knowing him to be a holy and righteous man.
—Mk 6:20

**APR.
27**

The power of a holy life

REFLECTION. What are you known for? Some men may answer this question pointing to an accomplishment in the workplace, at school, or with a sports team or other organization. There is nothing wrong with these, but they fall short of the standard that John the Baptist set.

Are you known for your faith, for your association with the Catholic Church, and for being a righteous man?

PRAYER. *St. John the Baptist, pray for me to be the man of God Jesus desires.*

COME away with me, by yourselves, to a deserted place and rest for a while.
—Mk 6:31

Go away!

REFLECTION. If it was important for Jesus to make time for some rest it's most likely important for us as well. As silly as it may sound, many men suffer from the delusion that the world can't get on without them.

Getting away or going on a retreat is important for the body, mind, and spirit.

PRAYER. *Jesus, You are the Savior and not I. May my vacations refresh me for the journey.*

HAVE courage! It is I! Do not be afraid!
—Mk 6:50

Never fear, Jesus is here!

REFLECTION. Time and time again Jesus offers His reassurance and calls His followers to have faith and courage. Jesus knows the fragility of the human condition.

What should give us confidence is the fact that Jesus is present. When Jesus states, "It is I," that should be enough for us. Does your presence instill that same sense of relief to others who look for guidance?

PRAYER. *Jesus, I can go forward with confidence because You are present in all things.*

PEOPLE out on the streets, they don't know who I am. —David Thomas

APR. 30

The poor may be closer than you think

REFLECTION. People can become isolated from others for a number of reasons. Physical disabilities, mental disease, and illness are but a few.

As Jesus was sent to seek and save the lost perhaps we can lead the way to reach out to those who may be disconnected from society. Are there any ministries in your parish that do this? If not, start one.

PRAYER. *Jesus, there are many needs in our society; use me to make a difference.*

ST. JOSEPH was constantly attentive to God, open to the signs of God's presence. —Pope Francis

MAY 1

In all things attentive

REFLECTION. St. Joseph was a man without words but not without witness. His silent witness makes us even more aware of his actions which occurred during one crises or another.

Like St. Joseph, we don't need words when actions will suffice. How can you develop your attentiveness to God's will to be a man of action in the mold of St. Joseph?

PRAYER. *St. Joseph, may your example of attentiveness inspire me to grow in holiness.*

67

CAN never find anything to say to God **MAY**
except: "Thy will be done." **2**
                                   —Malcolm Muggeridge

An abiding trust

REFLECTION. Malcolm Muggeridge was the man who brought Mother Teresa and her Sisters to the world through his book, *Something Beautiful for God*, in the late 1960s.

He had a difficult time asking God for specifics. After witnessing firsthand the total and absolute trust Mother Teresa placed in God's hands he knew that this simple prayer was enough.

PRAYER. *Heavenly Father, may my desire always be to do Your will in my life.*

T'S your Church Lord, I'm going to bed. **MAY**
                                   —Pope St. John XXIII **3**

We're the players, not the owner

REFLECTION. There is a certain pressure when you own a business, organization, or sports team. Owners make decisions that can set the trajectory of the organization for years to come.

Pope St. John XXIII has a simple yet beautiful perspective on the Church that he was leading. It speaks not of irresponsibility but of absolute trust in God whose Church it is.

PRAYER. *Jesus, may I be a faithful servant in Your Church.*

HO do you say that I am?" Peter answered him. "You are the Christ."
—Mk 8:29

A question for the ages

REFLECTION. Jesus spent a great deal of time with His disciples before He presents this crucial question to them. It is Peter who steps forward with the answer, "You are the Christ."

While Peter is far from perfect I admire his boldness and confidence in answering the question. How do you answer this question not only in your heart but in the "marketplace" as well?

PRAYER. *Lord Jesus, may I never be ashamed of You or my faith and trust in You.*

 E TOLD them these facts in plain words.
—Mk 8:32

Can't escape the Cross

REFLECTION. Jesus speaks to His disciples about His future arrest, suffering, and death in language that is plain and straightforward. It's a difficult message to deliver and His disciples don't want to hear it, but He tells them anyway.

The Cross and suffering are part of our discipleship, and while we don't look for suffering we must accept it. Christianity without the Cross is meaningless.

PRAYER. *Father, give me courage to accept the different crosses that I must carry.*

ANYONE who wishes to follow me must deny himself, take up his cross, and follow me. —Mk 8:34

MAY 6

Not an easy road

REFLECTION. At first glance denying yourself seems like a momentous proposition yet we do it all the time. We deny ourselves sleep, time, and money for the activities and people that we love.

When we say yes to one thing it usually means we deprive ourselves of others. Our yes to Jesus will mean denial yet great joy as well.

PRAYER. *Lord Jesus, help me to go where You lead and do so with joy.*

WHAT does it profit a man to gain the whole world and forfeit his very life? —Mk 8:36

MAY 7

Checking the balance sheet

REFLECTION. Sometimes faith has a very practical aspect to it for those who believe. We realize that there is a God and that we will be held accountable for the choices we made.

There is nothing wrong with wealth and the world's goods except when we place them before God and His law of love. Ill-gotten wealth has a high price.

PRAYER. *Just Lord, may my possessions and wealth be used for Your glory and for raising others up.*

JESUS took Peter, James, and John and led them up a high mountain apart by themselves. —Mk 9:2

MAY 8

Investing in relationships

REFLECTION. Jesus preached to the crowds, was followed by disciples, chose the twelve and invested all in Peter, James, and John. Jesus' method of transforming the world focused on small groups and in particular, these three Apostles.

Who has mentored or coached you along the way? Who are some men you admire who have invested themselves in you? To whom are you a model of faith?

PRAYER. *Jesus, thank You for showing me the way to help and be helped by others.*

THIS is my beloved Son. Listen to him. —Mk 9:7

MAY 9

The voice of God

REFLECTION. How often do people wish to hear the voice of God in a clear, direct manner? Often God communicates in small signs, through others, and in the silence of our heart.

The Gospel writer Mark records the clear, concise word of God, and the message is quite simple: "Listen to him." How can you take time each day to listen to Jesus?

PRAYER. *God our Father, what You ask is simple yet challenging. Help me hear Your Son's voice.*

ALL things are possible for one who has faith. —Mk 9:23

Don't limit God

REFLECTION. Jesus gives this response to a man whose son was possessed by a spirit which caused his son convulsions. We can only imagine the fear and discomfort this caused the father and the rest of the family.

Jesus' words are spirit and life and can bring about healing. It is Jesus in whom we place our trust, seeking His will and not our own.

PRAYER. *Jesus, make me a man of faith, trust, and a witness to Your love.*

DO NOT walk through time without leaving worthy evidence of your passage. —Pope St. John XXIII

One life to make a difference

REFLECTION. As a man gets older he begins to think of his legacy. A few of the extremely wealthy may have their legacy memorialized in hospital buildings or in universities.

For the rest of us, like Christ and the Saints, we can leave behind evidence of our life through the quality of our love for one another. It's all that matters.

PRAYER. *Loving God, may my legacy be rooted in Your love and lived out in faith.*

Y CONFIDENCE is placed in God who does not need our help for accomplishing his designs.

MAY 12

—St. Isaac Jogues

Get out of the way

REFLECTION. St. Isaac Jogues was one of the first martyrs on American soil. He and his companions gave their lives in teaching and sharing the Good News of Jesus.

When several of his fingers had been cut, chewed, or burnt off by the Huron Indians, St. Jogues could no longer say Mass. In the end he gave all for God.

PRAYER. *St. Isaac Jogues, pray for me that I may be as faithful as you were.*

 HERE there is peace and meditation, there is neither anxiety nor doubt. —St. Francis of Assisi

MAY 13

What drives out doubt?

REFLECTION. St. Francis offers wisdom on how to dispel anxiety and doubt and the remedy includes meditation. Meditation can assist us in focusing our heart and mind on Christ and His Word instead of what may be troubling us.

St. Paul gives similar advice in his letters. Have you ever meditated or simply sat in a quiet place to pray? Take time this week to do so.

PRAYER. *Jesus, assist my efforts to focus on You and to meditate on Your Word.*

UT you will receive power when the Holy Spirit comes upon you. —Acts 1:8

A promise of power

REFLECTION. A thirst for power is not new to the human experience. From antiquity, men have sought power and at times have done ruthless things to receive it.

The power Jesus offers is His own Spirit which empowers us to follow His way of love, mercy and justice. When you find it difficult to follow Jesus, ask for His power and He will provide it.

PRAYER. *Holy Spirit, empower me to be the man of God that You desire me to be.*

LL of these were constantly engaged in prayer. —Acts 1:14

Praying with heart, mind, and words

REFLECTION. When the Apostles and Mary were gathered together in the Upper Room before the feast of Pentecost, they were engaged in prayer. In the same way that a car can't move forward until the gears are engaged so too with the Christian life.

When we engage God through prayer it has the power to effect change and get us going in the right direction.

PRAYER. *Jesus, may my prayer life be consistent and focused, fully engaged in Your will.*

FOR he must become a witness with us of his resurrection.

—Acts 1:22

MAY
16

Hear, see, and touch

REFLECTION. After the death of Judas, the Apostles needed another eyewitness to replace him. The key criteria, along with being present to the life and ministry of Jesus, was that he was to be a witness to the Resurrection.

The Church still needs witnesses to the Resurrection of Jesus who share that witness with those who have not yet encountered Christ.

PRAYER. *Lord God, send me to be Your witness at home, at work, and wherever I go.*

MEN of Israel, hear these words.

—Acts 2:22

MAY
17

From the mouth of a fisherman

REFLECTION. Early on in the ministry of Jesus He told Peter, "Follow me and I will make you fishers of men." After the descent of the Holy Spirit Peter is empowered to start fishing. Not for fish, but as Jesus said, for men.

What was the lure Peter used? He used his own witness and the Word of God. Can you articulate your witness?

PRAYER. *My Lord, forgive me those times I have failed to witness to You before others.*

GOD raised this Jesus to life. Of that we are all witnesses. —Acts 2:32

An honest testimony

REFLECTION. Without the Resurrection, Jesus would have been a footnote in history. However, God raised Him from the dead.

The Christian witness is comprised not of facts and figures but of witness to our encounter with the living Lord who has changed our lives, forgiven our sins, and given us the promise of eternal life. Others will believe on account of your witness.

PRAYER. *Mary, be a mother to me and pray that I may be a fearless witness to Jesus.*

ACT today in such a way that you need not blush tomorrow. —St. John Bosco

Be a man of your word...and actions!

REFLECTION. It's remarkable how diligent reporters can be when researching the past behavior of those who run for political office. It seems everything a candidate did and said, even going back to high school, is fair game.

As Christians we admit we are sinners and that we make mistakes. We should take the advice of St. John Bosco, however, and think before we act.

PRAYER. *Lord, forgive me for my imprudence and guide me in wise actions.*

THEY devoted themselves to the teaching of the apostles and to the communal fellowship, the breaking of bread and to prayers. —Acts 2:42

Blueprint for successful ministry

REFLECTION. There are many different models for how a small Christian community should be run. The best model is, however, the one presented in the Word of God in which we read of these four essential elements.

Each one is necessary for authentic Christian discipleship to take place. Do you experience all four? Which one may be lacking in your life?

PRAYER. *Jesus, may I be devoted to all four of these practices and grow in my love for You.*

AND day by day the Lord added to those who were being saved. —Acts 2:47

What is it to be saved?

REFLECTION. Catholics can get confused and defensive when asked the question: "Are you saved?"

It's not in our Catholic vocabulary to speak this way, but as Catholics we can be confident in our salvation but also realize that we can jeopardize it. Our salvation is contingent upon many things according to Scripture such as our actions and God's mercy.

PRAYER. *Lord, grant me confidence in Your mercy, and give me strength to follow You.*

DEVOTION must be exercised in different ways by the gentleman, the workman, the servant, the prince.

MAY 22

—St. Francis de Sales

Give glory to God whatever your vocation

REFLECTION. St. Francis de Sales is known for his book, *The Devout Life*. His writing was groundbreaking for its time because he recognized and encouraged sanctity and holiness for the lay person.

Holiness is not reserved for clergy alone but for all of the baptized. Have you ever considered your call to holiness in your state of life?

PRAYER. *Lord Jesus, may I be a saint as a husband, father, and in the workplace.*

TO LISTEN at prayer is to take the chance of hearing the voice of Christ in the poor, the weak, those whom we love and those whom we do not love.

MAY 23

—Fr. Benedict Groeschel

Listening with intention

REFLECTION. It's amazing how much "noise" our heart, mind, and ears have to filter each day. Numerous commercials and messages from friends and others come our way.

Have you ever intently listened to another or even suggested that you go somewhere to speak to get away from the noise? Can you intentionally listen to God each day?

PRAYER. *Jesus, attune my ears and heart to Your voice each and every day.*

BY FAITH in his name, this man whom you see here and who is known to you has been made strong. —Acts 3:16

We can all be this man

REFLECTION. St. Peter was talking about a man who was physically healed by the name of Jesus. It's true that we are all that man! We, who believe in the name of Jesus, have been forgiven and strengthened by the Holy Spirit for our own unique mission.

Is your faith "known to all?" Will you be a witness to all the good God has done for you?

PRAYER. *Come Holy Spirit, empower me to be a man of God at all times in all places.*

THEY were amazed to see the fearlessness shown by Peter and John. —Acts 4:13

MAY 25

Uneducated and ordinary men

REFLECTION. The crowd was amazed by Peter and John and in this instance their amazement focuses on the fearlessness of these two men. It seems that faith and fearlessness do make a powerful combination.

When have you been both faithful and fearless as a disciple of Jesus? Have you ever prayed in public, or tried to right an injustice?

PRAYER. *Heavenly Father, forgive me those times I have been cowardly in living the faith.*

E CANNOT possibly refrain from speaking about what we have seen and heard. —Acts 4:20

MAY 26

Compelled to speak out

REFLECTION. In the same way that faith cannot be forced upon another person, speaking about faith cannot be compelled either. Yet, for those who have encountered the personal forgiveness and love of Jesus Christ silence is not an option.

Many Christians have been put to death for speaking about their faith not because they hated this life; they just loved Christ more.

PRAYER. *Lord, may I never be ashamed to speak about my faith in You.*

N THE ordinary providence of your everyday lives, you are the Church and you have the grace. —Fr. Thomas A. Judge

MAY 27

You have all that you need

REFLECTION. Fr. Thomas A. Judge was a man ahead of his time. Early in the 1900s he envisioned a laity who, if empowered, could be a powerful force in the Church and in the world.

His motto, "Every Catholic an Apostle" is as true today as it was back then. Each of us is called to be good, do good, and be a power for good wherever God calls us.

PRAYER. *Jesus, may I remember that I am a part of the Body of Christ and called to do my part.*

THEY were all filled with the Holy Spirit and proclaimed the word of God fearlessly. —Acts 4:31

MAY 28

Heavenly connections

REFLECTION. The Holy Spirit is mentioned over one hundred times in the Acts of the Apostles and each time the Spirit is mentioned He is empowering people for witness. Seventy-five percent of those times the witness is verbal.

The Spirit empowers people to teach, prophesy, proclaim, preach, and even to pray in tongues. Speaking of faith is an outward sign that the Spirit is in you.

PRAYER. *Lord God, send Your Holy Spirit to empower me to witness to Your love.*

THE entire community of believers was united in heart and soul. —Acts 4:32

MAY 29

A sign to the world

REFLECTION. The picture of the early Christian community seems almost too good to be true. We read that they shared their possessions and divided their belongings so that no one would be in need.

While it's easy to point fingers and criticize those who don't share their goods and who divide communities, we will have to answer for our own generosity. What gifts can you share?

PRAYER. *Mary, pray for me to be as generous as you were in giving to others.*

ITH great power, the apostles bore witness to the resurrection of the Lord Jesus, and they were all greatly respected. —Acts 4:33

MAY 30

Power, witness, and respect

REFLECTION. Most men are fortunate to have a "great" man in their lives who they admire and respect. Respect is one of those words men aspire to for at the end of the day we seek the respect of our family, children, and peers.

As important as praise and respect can be from others, ultimately we should desire to be men of God for that in turn, gets respect.

PRAYER. *God Almighty, may my first desire be to do Your will.*

HEY say they've got control of you, but that's not true you know. —Jake Burns

MAY 31

We have a choice

REFLECTION. Life is not always easy and the choices we face can seem to be a choice between two evils. We also may feel pressured in certain situations to act in a way that's not compatible with the Gospel and with our conscience.

During these times we need to pray and trust in the wise counsel of others who can help us along the way.

PRAYER. *Jesus, into Your hands I commend my life trusting in Your love for me.*

OD looked at everything he had made, and he found it very good. —Gen 1:31

In the beginning it's all good

REFLECTION. Sometimes we can get upset and frustrated at the way things turn out. Even the best of plans can go awry and the meticulous and time-consuming preparation seems wasted.

It's good to remember that God's original plan was for good. It seems simple but it's true. God can bring about good under any circumstances.

PRAYER. *Lord, help me to remember that Your plan is what's best all the time.*

HE Lord God said: "It is not good for man to be alone. I will make a suitable partner for him." —Gen 2:18

What's not good?

REFLECTION. The author of Genesis repeats the phrase, "It was good," multiple times in the creation account. Here, however, we read of one thing not being good and that's the original solitude.

Perhaps God created Adam first so he could experience this "original solitude" and thus appreciate the gift of Eve and the family that would follow. Many years later it's still not good to be isolated from others.

PRAYER. *My God, thank You for the family, friends, and people in my life who make it complete.*

ID God really tell you not to eat from any of the trees in the garden?

—Gen 3:1

Seeds of doubt

REFLECTION. Ah Satan, that great deceiver! In studying the technique of Satan we can gain insight into his methods when dealing with men. It seems that he tries to plant the seed of doubt in what God has clearly stated.

How may we hear Satan's voice today? When we hear "If God loves you" or "Does God really forgive your sin?" it is not the voice of God!

PRAYER. *St. Michael, attune my ears to God's voice and protect me from the evil one.*

HE Lord God then called to the man and asked him: "Where are you?"

—Gen 3:9

Still a good question to ponder

REFLECTION. We get the idea that walking in the garden was a regular occurrence for God. When He asks, "Where are you?" it is not a directional question but a relational one. God is really asking "where are you in relationship to Me?"

In asking the question Adam realizes the distance that sin places between himself and God. Where are you in your relationship with God?

PRAYER. *Merciful Lord, may I never stray from You, and may I remain close in good times and bad.*

FOR the man and his wife the Lord God made leather garments, with which he clothed them. —Gen 3:21

5

Banished but cared for

REFLECTION. This short verse reveals a great deal about the love of God. Even though the man and woman turned their backs on God He did not abandon them but rather provided for them.

There are consequences for sin, but it did not remove God's love for Adam and Eve or for us. As a man, do you withhold your love and care from those who may reject you?

PRAYER. *God, help me to love as You love and not to count the cost.*

BUT Noah found favor with the Lord. —Gen 6:8

JUNE

6

God takes notice

REFLECTION. In the midst of the wickedness of humanity we are told that Noah found favor with God. We further read that he was righteous, blameless, and that he walked with God.

It can be frustrating to feel as if you're the only one trying to please God and do the right thing as I'm sure it was in Noah's day. Remember, God takes notice.

PRAYER. *Just Lord, may I always be found upright and blameless in my conduct.*

OAH complied; he did just as God had commanded him. —Gen 6:22 **JUNE 7**

It's faithfulness that matters

REFLECTION. Think of all the ways that people are judged. Their physical appearance, their career, the town they live in, the car they drive, and the list goes on.

God judges not as humans do. God looks at the heart and asks for faithfulness. God asked Noah to build a boat in the desert and he complied. When God asks us to do the ridiculous. . . the miraculous follows.

PRAYER. *Heavenly Father, help me discern Your will, and give me the fortitude to live it out.*

 BRAM went as the Lord directed him, and Lot went with him. —Gen 12:4 **JUNE 8**

Name changer

REFLECTION. We find Abram, (who had his name changed to Abraham) early on in the book of Genesis. Like Noah before him, he is obedient even at an advanced age. He knows not where this journey will lead, but he sets out with his nephew Lot to a strange land.

Do you take time to listen to God and allow Him to guide your steps?

PRAYER. *Heavenly Father, guide my steps and attune my ear to Your voice.*

THEN Abram journeyed on by stages to the Negeb. —Gen 12:9

Stages of growth

REFLECTION. The Negeb is one of the distinctive deserts in the Middle East, and the terrain is stark and desolate. It is here that Abram journeyed in stages.

How often do we expect God to lead us directly to the "promised land" without any hardships along the way? While God is unpredictable, He is never unfaithful. Realize that we are not yet at our final destination.

PRAYER. *Lord God, give me enough light and strength to journey forward.*

IS ANYTHING too marvelous for the Lord to do? —Gen 18:14

Where is your faith?

REFLECTION. Abraham's wife Sarah is told that she will give birth and her response is laughter because in her own words she describes herself as; "worn out" and her husband as "old."

What seems impossible for us is not impossible for God. We all have situations which require the "marvelous" intervention of God. Ask, pray, and listen and see how the Lord moves.

PRAYER. *Jesus, may my confidence in You and Your will be reflected in my prayers.*

HIS is the very perfection of a man, to find out his own imperfections.

—St. Augustine

Humility and honesty

REFLECTION. To be told that we have imperfections is both obvious and a bit humbling. Before others have the opportunity to call us out on our failing, the advice of St. Augustine is fitting.

Self-examination is good and indeed necessary to advance in the spiritual life. Take some time to reflect on areas of your life where you need God's grace to change.

PRAYER. *Jesus, examine me and lead me on the way of perfection.*

RAY, hope, and don't worry.

—St. Pio of Pietrelcina

Safe and secure

REFLECTION. If our future is not rooted in our belief in God then what will naturally follow is worry. We have all experienced fear and anxiety in our lives in various degrees, but our faith informs us that God is ultimately in control.

The degree to which we worry is the degree to which we trust God. Live the advice of St. Pio!

PRAYER. *Lord, what You ask for is humble, childlike faith. Help my unbelief!*

OD gives each one of us sufficient grace ever to know His holy will, and to do it fully. —St. Ignatius of Loyola

JUNE 13

His grace is enough

REFLECTION. St. Ignatius assures us that God provides grace so we may know His will. Most often knowing God's will does not occur through a flash of lightning or the sound of thunder but over time with reassurances along the way.

Through the discipline of prayer, counsel, and discernment God communicates His will to us. Ask for the grace to know His will and to do it.

PRAYER. *Lord, reach me in a way that I know You are speaking to me.*

 UT we possess the mind of Christ. —1 Cor 2:16

JUNE 14

Think like the Master

REFLECTION. An apprentice walks in the shadow of the master craftsman in order to learn how things are done in many fields of work. In doing so the student not only learns the trade but how the master thinks, anticipates, and resolves problems.

In our discipleship, we, too, need to follow Christ closely to study how He loved and to think like He does.

PRAYER. *Jesus, help me to stay close to You as I seek to learn Your ways.*

89

FOR we are God's coworkers; you are God's field, God's building. —1 Cor 3:9

We belong to God

REFLECTION. St. Paul writes to the Christians in the city of Corinth instructing them that they and the apostles all belong to God. While each one has a different ministry or gift, working together we make up "God's field" or "God's building."

Whatever metaphor St. Paul uses it's clear that God is the focus, and we assist in accomplishing His will.

PRAYER. *Lord God, help me to focus on what is most essential this day.*

DO YOU not realize that you are God's temple, and that the Spirit of God dwells in you? —1 Cor 3:16

Your heart is God's home

REFLECTION. To some people we are merely flesh and blood, here today and gone tomorrow.

Christians however, take another view because of God's Word which indicates that God's Holy Spirit dwells in each of us. This should impact not only how we see ourselves but how we view everyone for we are all created in the image and likeness of God.

PRAYER. *Come Holy Spirit, stir up Your Spirit within me to radiate God's loving presence.*

APPEAL to you then to be imitators of me. **JUNE 17**
—1 Cor 4:16

A bold statement indeed!

REFLECTION. St. Paul was a Christian and a man called apart to proclaim the Good News of Jesus Christ. He utters these remarkable words, "be imitators of me." What a shining example of Christ St. Paul must have been in order to utter those words.

Can you utter those same words to those who are learning about Jesus? What kind of example are you providing?

PRAYER. *St. Paul, pray for me that I may be a worthy witness to Christ.*

 OR the Kingdom of God is not a matter of words but of power. **JUNE 18**
—1 Cor 4:20

God works through our weakness

REFLECTION. Power is not usually associated with Christianity. Forgiveness, mercy, and love are most likely the words that a Catholic will call to mind when discussing Jesus and the Church.

Perhaps our understanding of power and Jesus' understanding are not in tune. For it is in forgiveness, mercy, and love that we find and experience the power of God in our world.

PRAYER. *Mary, be a mother to me and help me unleash the power of your Son's love wherever I go.*

RE you not aware that wrongdoers will never inherit the kingdom of God? —1 Cor 6:9 **JUNE 19**

Only God can judge you and He will

REFLECTION. An inheritance is a gift received and not something earned. The gift of Heaven awaits those who are faithful to Christ.

It can be sobering to realize that this inheritance can be lost through our apostasy or renunciation of our faith. It can also be lost through our actions which fall under the realm of mortal sin. God will be just.

PRAYER. *Lord, use whatever means necessary to guide me on the way to Heaven.*

 ISTEN and attend with the ear of your heart. —St. Benedict **JUNE 20**

Trust your intuition

REFLECTION. We have all been on the other side of a sales pitch where all the facts and figures lined up but still something just didn't "feel" right. Whether or not intuition can be scientifically proven we have all experienced that uneasy feeling inside of us.

Sometimes God operates through that same intuition that tells us to go for it or to steer clear. Be attuned to God's call.

PRAYER. *Jesus, help my heart to be pure so I may attune it to Your voice.*

FOUND out that if you are going to win games, you had better be ready to adapt.

JUNE 21

—Scotty Bowman

Game plan adjustment

REFLECTION. Scotty Bowman is one of the most successful coaches of all time winning nine Stanley Cup Championships with three different teams. In professional sports as in life, you don't know what obstacles, injuries, or tragedies are right around the corner.

We too, must be ready to adapt to changing situations not only to win games but to live as faith-filled men.

PRAYER. *My God, assist me in adapting to life's changing circumstances.*

 HOSE who want to find their joy in externals all too easily grow empty themselves.

JUNE 22

—St. Augustine

Made for more

REFLECTION. Catholics are certainly called to enjoy the external pleasures of life. Food, drink, and all that satiates the body are indeed good. The mistake is in thinking that those externals can satiate our deepest needs and desires.

We are spiritual beings and are made for more. As St. Augustine would learn himself, our hearts are indeed restless until they rest in Him.

PRAYER. *St. Augustine, pray for me to be the man God desires me to be.*

93

OSES listened to his father-in-law and did all that he had said.
—Ex 18:24

JUNE 23

Humble enough to listen

REFLECTION. Success and victory can do strange things to a man's ego. We can gradually, or sometimes overnight, start to believe that we are the one that the sun revolves around when we have had a major conquest professionally or personally.

Moses was God's servant and through Moses the waters were parted and the Israelites freed. Still, Moses sought and took advice from others.

PRAYER. *Lord God, may I be humble enough to seek Your will through the counsel of others.*

UT Moses led the people out of the camp to meet God.
—Ex 19:17

JUNE 24

Leaders lead

REFLECTION. Moses was a natural born leader. First he led sheep then he led men. Much like the early disciples who were called to be fishers of men Moses led people to God.

We are told that Moses was not perfect which is comforting, but at the end of the day he led others to God. In the resume that you have established over the years have you led anyone to God?

PRAYER. *Almighty God, may my prayers and witness lead others to You.*

O MOSES went down to the people to speak to them. —Ex 19:25

JUNE 25

Speak to God first

REFLECTION. Moses first speaks to God before he speaks to the people. How often do we pray before we speak at an important meeting?

Speaking to God first may not change the other person, but it will certainly change us and allow us to see a person created in the image and likeness of God in front of us.

PRAYER. *Lord, may I speak to You before I speak to others to ensure a positive conversation.*

OU shall not follow the crowd in doing wrong. —Ex 23:2

JUNE 26

Crowd pleaser or God pleaser

REFLECTION. Following a crowd is not wrong in itself, but to resist the crowd when they are doing wrong is the real challenge. In today's day and age we are not talking about picking up rocks and stoning someone, but the allure of following the crowd is still strong.

The question becomes who are you following and will you have the fortitude not to follow those who do wrong.

PRAYER. *Jesus, may my conscience be formed so correctly that I can avoid evil.*

WHAT a player does best, he should practice the least. Practice is for problems. —Duke Snider

JUNE 27

Fill in the gaps

REFLECTION. The iconic Brooklyn Dodger baseball player Duke Snider offers some sound advice to those who play baseball. Work on your weaknesses!

In the spiritual life we can take a page from his philosophy and work on those areas which we need to grow in. Humility, service, patience, and any number of virtues can all be areas which we can work on in order to be more like Christ.

PRAYER. *Holy Spirit, reveal to me those areas that I need to work on in my own life.*

THE priest shall burn this on the altar as food, an oblation to the Lord. —Lev 3:11

JUNE 28

Give your very best

REFLECTION. Throughout the Book of Leviticus we read of sacrifices, oblations, and of practices which seem far removed from current practices. Yet when we read of the meticulous nature of the sacrifice—the fat around the lobe of the kidney and liver—we discover that when you give to God, you give your very best.

How can you more faithfully give your best to God?

PRAYER. *Lord, help me give my very best to You as I see Your face in those I meet each day.*

TO CONVERT somebody go and take them by the hand and guide them.

—St. Thomas Aquinas

JUNE 29

The gift of accompaniment

REFLECTION. Every teacher is aware that students retain little of what they hear, some of what they see, but most of what they are actively engaged in. So too with discipleship. People would rather see a sermon than to hear one.

Who has assisted you on your journey of faith? How can you be actively engaged in assisting someone to be a man of Christ?

PRAYER. *Jesus, the Good Shepherd, thank You for those who have taught me about You.*

MY perfect cousin, what I like to do he doesn't.

—Michael Bradley

JUNE 30

The families golden boy

REFLECTION. When a person grows up surrounded by a large family including neighboring cousins there can be some favoritism exhibited now and again which can give rise to envy and jealousy.

Not to make excuses for those who show favoritism, but like everything in life it can be a cause for reflection. Are we just in our judgments? Do we show favoritism?

PRAYER. *Lord Jesus, may I treat everyone with fairness and dignity this day and always.*

EHOLD, he is coming in the clouds; every eye will see him, even those who pierced him.
—Rev 1:7

He will come again

REFLECTION. People have different responses to the fact that Christ will come again. Some look forward to the event with great longing and excitement, others perhaps with some fear and trepidation, and still others would categorize His return as a fairy tale.

Jesus did not mince words when He said He would come again. What is your response to Christ's return?

PRAYER. *Lord, may I wait expectantly for Your return with joy and anticipation.*

AM also aware of your perseverance and how you have toiled for my name without becoming weary.
—Rev 2:3

Finishing strong

REFLECTION. In the Book of Revelation we read the encouraging words written to the church in Ephesus. Often we get in a groove and that groove becomes a rut.

It seems that the Ephesians were living the faith and trying their best to do all for Jesus. They are indeed running the "good race" of faith without giving up. How are you running your race?

PRAYER. *Lord, help me not to grow weary but to finish strong as a man of faith.*

HOWEVER, I have this complaint against you: you have lost the love you had at first. —Rev 2:4

JULY 3

Don't go breaking my heart

REFLECTION. The Ephesians are praised for staying the course but it would seem that the Lord is looking for more than just laborers and workers. He is looking for men who love Him, who understand His life, and sacrifice joyfully for the Kingdom of God.

Only through spending time with the one we love will our love grow. What is your time commitment each day to Jesus?

PRAYER. *Lord, may my faith never be a matter of just "mailing it in." Draw me closer to You.*

 I KNOW your deeds. You have a reputation for being alive, but you are dead. —Rev 3:1

JULY 4

Glory days

REFLECTION. Any athlete will tell you that they are only as good as their last game. Past home-runs and touchdowns were nice but: "what have you done for me lately!"

In our life of faith we know that our soul is at stake and that is infinitely more valuable than any sports award. Is your faith growing day by day or are you living in the past?

PRAYER. *Come Holy Spirit, may my joy arise from my living relationship with Christ.*

KNOW your deeds, that you are neither cold nor hot. **JULY 5** —Rev 3:15

Are you all in?

REFLECTION. There is a story about the NY Giants football team that before a game which would determine if they qualified for the play-offs, a guest speaker gave each player a poker chip.

After his speech he asked the team if they were ready to go "all in" or if they were going to play it safe and hold onto the chip. Are you all in for Christ?

PRAYER. *Jesus, I am all in for You! May I never hold anything back from You.*

 S IT is, as you are lukewarm, neither cold nor hot, I will spit you out of my mouth. **JULY 6** —Rev 3:16

Go big or go home

REFLECTION. Any business professional or coach will tell you that they would rather have five committed people on their team who are willing to give 100% of themselves rather than one hundred people who are lukewarm.

Jesus is clear on this as well. He loves us as we are, but if we are to make an impact for Christ in this world He needs us to be committed.

PRAYER. *Lord, I'm committed to so many things that are not as important as my faith. Help me to be a man of God.*

EHOLD, I am standing at the door, knocking. —Rev 3:20

JULY 7

He never grows weary

REFLECTION. The knocking that Christ does is on the door of our heart. He may not always knock loudly, and He'll never force His way in, yet He continues to knock.

It may be easy to ignore some people in our lives or to block an unwanted phone call, but the love of Jesus compels Him to knock. Have you opened your heart to Him and let Him in?

PRAYER. *Jesus, attune my heart to Your patient and gentle knocking.*

 ET us never forget that authentic power is service. —Pope Francis

JULY 8

Upside down world

REFLECTION. Believing in Jesus Christ does turn a man's world and world view upside down. The "world" would have us believe that all the power is in the hands of the people rich enough to buy it. God's perspective and the example of Jesus tell another story.

Who has served and cared about you? That is real power.

PRAYER. *Lord, may my life be guided and transformed by Your word.*

HE Christian ideal has not been tried and found wanting. It has been found difficult; and left untried.

—G. K. Chesterton

Are you strong enough?

REFLECTION. Christianity is not for wimps. If you think it's easy following Jesus and forgiving your enemies, turning the other cheek, going the extra mile, and having the discipline to pray then you've never tried it.

The discipline and commitment are worth it however, and those who do live a life bound to Christ know its rewards.

PRAYER. *My Lord and God, may I never waiver in my commitment to You.*

 ASTING detaches you from this world. Prayer reattaches you to the next world.

—Archbishop Fulton Sheen

Detach to attach

REFLECTION. Usually the idea of fasting comes around only during Lent for most Catholics. It is a practice that is not limited to Lent however, and the small sacrifices we make every day allow us not just to detach from a meal.

Fasting calls us to attach, cling, or cleave to Jesus so to realize that this world is not all there is. Heaven awaits!

PRAYER. *Lord Jesus, may my thoughts, words, and prayers remind me I am created for You.*

OR you, the most beautiful moment is the present moment. Live it full of love for God.
—Cardinal Thuan

A taste of Heaven

REFLECTION. God is in the present moment. Yet how often do we spend energy and time looking backward and forward worrying ourselves to death about things beyond our control.

The advice from Cardinal Thuan is perfect for he spent 13 years in prison for being Catholic, and nine of those years were spent in solitary confinement. Find God in this present moment.

PRAYER. *Jesus, help me to focus on my responsibilities in this present moment for You are here.*

 HE smoke of the incense together with the prayers of the saints rose before God.
—Rev 8:4

Meeting of Heaven and earth

REFLECTION. The vison that St. John shares with us from the Book of Revelation is familiar to Catholics because we experience what is recorded in Heaven at each Mass. The Lamb of God is present, the choirs of angels, candles, incense and praise, worship and thanksgiving.

How do you prepare yourself for this awesome event? How can you enter more fully into Mass?

PRAYER. *Lord God Almighty, I praise You and worship You for You are the Lord.*

HEN another scroll was opened, the book of life, and the dead were judged according to their deeds. —Rev 20:12

A little less talk and a little more action

REFLECTION. The Book of Revelation makes it crystal clear that there is a Heaven, there will be a judgment, and that our deeds are the criteria on which we will be judged.

Faith is a verb so it is not just an intellectual assent to certain truths but how we live those truths in the providence of our daily lives that matters. Be a man of faith. . . in action.

PRAYER. *Hail Mary, assist me in living out my faith with intention and vigor.*

EHOLD, I am making all things new. —Rev 21:5

The power of God

REFLECTION. Change, as we all know, can be difficult. It can also be a welcome guest. Old ways of doing things give way to faster and easier ways.

Imagine how different your life would be if you lived one hundred years ago. The changes in travel, medicine, technology, and literacy have improved the lives of millions. It is impossible to imagine the power God has to change us.

PRAYER. *Holy Spirit, renew me and form me into the man You desire.*

THE light shines in the darkness, and the darkness has been unable to overcome it. —Jn 1:5

You are the light

REFLECTION. In scripture fire and light represent the presence of God. Jesus, the true light of the world, came into the world and the darkness of sin and the human condition were unable to overcome Him.

Jesus calls us to be the light, the presence of God, in our families, in our workplace, and in the world. Follow Jesus and you will not walk in darkness.

PRAYER. *Merciful Father, let the light of faith shine through me as I follow You.*

HE CAME as a witness to give testimony to the light, so that through him all might come to believe. —Jn 1:7

You have one job

REFLECTION. John the Baptist had a unique role in relationship to Jesus and that was to point others to Christ. He gave his witness and testimony about who Jesus is.

We who are baptized Catholics are called to follow John the Baptist's example of giving testimony to Christ. When we encounter Jesus in a personal way we will be compelled to lead others to Him.

PRAYER. *St. John the Baptist, pray for me to lead other men to Jesus.*

E HIMSELF was not the light; his role was to bear witness to the light.

—Jn 1:8

JULY 17

How do we bear witness?

REFLECTION. The word "witness" is usually associated with the legal community and court proceedings. However, a witness is simply someone who can testify to what they have seen, heard, or been present for.

Catholics may not use this word frequently but we should be able to articulate our own personal encounter with Jesus Christ. Are you ready to bear witness?

PRAYER. *Holy Spirit, Advocate, help me to be bold in my testimony of who You are in my life.*

ND the Word became flesh and dwelt among us

—Jn 1:14

JULY 18

How do you live in the midst of others?

REFLECTION. The saying goes, "I'd rather see a sermon than hear one." The point being is that people tend to remember and recall what others did rather than only what they say.

God almighty humbled Himself and took the form of a human, one of us, to show us how to live and love. God was on display in Jesus. God is also on display through you.

PRAYER. *Lord, may my actions reflect Your Holy Spirit living in me.*

106

ROM his fullness we have all received, grace upon grace. —Jn 1:16

Grace flows from Him

REFLECTION. Jesus is not a new Moses who delivers a new law for He is God. The old covenant which was a gift to the chosen people is replaced not through the blood of bulls and sheep but through the sacrifice of Jesus.

God is clear that He chooses all of us to enter into His friendship. This is grace, to be accepted as a son of God.

PRAYER. *Jesus, thank You for the graces You pour out on me and my family.*

EHOLD the Lamb of God, who takes away the sin of the world. —Jn 1:29

The function of the lamb

REFLECTION. Identifying Jesus as a "lamb" sounds peculiar to us even though we proclaim this in our liturgy.

The lamb was what God commanded to be sacrificed during the Passover. To be identified as a lamb was to have your fate sealed. Yet this is why Jesus came--to be the perfect, unblemished sacrifice for sin. May we give our lives for others in the same way.

PRAYER. *Jesus, Lamb of God, may I be a man who lays down his life for others.*

HAT are you looking for?

—Jn 1:38

JULY
21

Great questions

REFLECTION. It's been my experience that good teachers have good answers but exceptional teachers ask great questions. There is no greater teacher than Jesus Christ and He asked some extraordinary questions that are still relevant.

What are YOU looking for? Is Jesus enough to satiate your deepest desires? Can any created thing ever be enough?

PRAYER. *Jesus, lead me deeper into the chambers of Your Sacred Heart.*

OME and see.

—Jn 1:39

JULY
22

An invitation and a promise

REFLECTION. In response to the questions posed by Jesus, two disciples of John the Baptist inquire as to where Jesus is staying. This is a way of indicating that they wish to be Jesus' disciples, His followers.

Jesus' answer contains an invitation and a promise. How have you responded to Jesus' invitation to come and see? His invitation to meet Him in the Eucharist?

PRAYER. *Merciful Jesus, may I always seek You. Surprise me often by Your love.*

THE first thing Andrew did was to seek out his brother Simon. **JULY** —Jn 1:41 **23**

Always bringing others to Jesus

REFLECTION. St. Andrew is only mentioned a few times in the Gospels, yet he is very consistent in his actions for he is always bringing someone to Jesus. He first brings his brother, then a little boy with loaves and fish, and finally he brings some people who speak only Greek to Jesus. Not a bad activity to be remembered for!

Who has brought you to Jesus?

PRAYER. *St. Andrew, pray that I may bring others to Jesus as you did.*

ENCOUNTERING Philip, he said to him, "Follow me." **JULY** —Jn 1:43 **24**

Invitation accepted

REFLECTION. Jesus was not afraid to make an invitation. Throughout the Gospels we hear Him say, "follow me," and men leave absolutely everything behind to follow Jesus.

While we can imagine what the voice of Jesus may have sounded like and the tone of His voice, the fact is He is still calling men to follow Him today. In the end, it's all that matters.

PRAYER. *St. Philip, pray that I may have my heart and ears attuned to the voice of Jesus.*

IS mother said to the servants," Do whatever he tells you." **JULY 25** —Jn 2:5

Famous last words

REFLECTION. The first miracle of Jesus was precipitated by the words of Mary, His Mother. The servers in fact do what Jesus says and a miracle occurs. These servers did the ridiculous and witnessed the miraculous.

As a disciple of Jesus we are called to do whatever He tells us which means we must be attentive to the Holy Spirit and to His words which are recorded in scripture.

PRAYER. *Mary, Mother of our Lord, assist me in doing whatever Jesus calls me to do.*

OR God did not send his Son into the world to condemn the world but in order that the world might be saved through him. **JULY 26** —Jn 3:17

Mercy is His mission

REFLECTION. The clear intention of God the Father is that all people come into a saving relationship with Him through Jesus. This is the reason why Jesus came: to save us.

If we decide not to accept the free gift of eternal life or we turn away from Christ then it is we who choose to be separated from God, not He from us.

PRAYER. *Our Father, as You sent Jesus, so send me to announce Your love and mercy.*

HE MUST increase; I must decrease.
—Jn 3:30

27

The role of every Catholic

REFLECTION. John the Baptist realized whose presence he was in when Jesus began His public ministry. John's role of pointing to Jesus was complete and it was time for Jesus to take center stage.

In our own discipleship we must die to self, die to our ego, die to sin, in order that Christ may come alive in us. Allow His light to shine through you.

PRAYER. *Lord, dying to myself is painful! Help me be a man who is full of Your Spirit.*

MY FOOD is to do the will of the one who sent me, and to accomplish his work.
—Jn 4:34

JULY
28

Getting the job done

REFLECTION. Most men have the experience of working at various jobs both during high school and beyond. At the end of the work week is the much anticipated and deserved paycheck.

Happy the man who loves what he does for he never really "works" a day in his life. Doing God's will does bring an inexplicable joy that is difficult to describe.

PRAYER. *Lord, may my service to You be done with joy and never begrudgingly.*

NLESS you witness signs and wonders, you will not believe. —Jn 4:48

Is His word enough?

REFLECTION. A royal official approaches Jesus with a request. He asks Jesus to come to his home in order to heal his son. Jesus makes this statement about seeing signs and wonders and then tells the man to go home for his son will live.

The man does as Jesus says, trusting in His word before he knows if his son is healed. Trust in Jesus' word and begin walking.

PRAYER. *Jesus, I trust in You regardless of any apparent signs or wonders.*

O YOU want to get well? —Jn 5:6

What really satisfies the soul?

REFLECTION. The question Jesus poses to a man who has been sick for 38 years seems ridiculous at first glance: "Do you want to get well?" The obvious answer is yes although the sick man complains about the pool.

While there is nothing wrong with pools or other material things our ultimate healing lies in our relationship with God through Jesus Christ.

PRAYER. *My God, thank You for stopping to help the sick man and me as well.*

RUNNING out of time again, where did you go wrong this time? —Bill Stevenson

JULY
31

We've all gone the wrong way at times

REFLECTION. It can be heartbreaking to see someone we love make bad decisions. We may give counsel and guidance as men who care, but ultimately people choose their own way.

While we may be tempted to give up hope and descend into despair, remember that we were all in the same boat until Christ saved us. In Christ there is always hope!

PRAYER. *Jesus our hope, may I never lose hope nor give into despair.*

SIR, I have no one to put me into the pool when the water is stirred up. —Jn 5:7

AUG.
1

Perhaps the saddest words in scripture

REFLECTION. In the Holy Land of Israel, in the shadow of the great Temple where Gods' glory shines forth we find a man who utters the words, "I have no one."

I wonder, "why didn't the people do something for him?" My thoughts then turn to myself and my actions. As a man, have I taken leadership in helping others?

PRAYER. *Jesus, may I seize opportunities to be proactive in helping others.*

113

CT today in such a way that you need not blush tomorrow. —St. John Bosco

AUG.
2

The patron of youth

REFLECTION. St. John Bosco offered some sound advice to young people. It still holds up today and is a sign of Christian maturity for it takes discipline and prudence to act in a manner worthy of Christ.

Those who live or work with young people can correct them, but our actions should be such that we can hold our head high because we acted out of a sense of justice and charity.

PRAYER. *St. John Bosco, pray for me and guide me in how I respond to others.*

HOEVER hears my words and believes in the one who sent me possesses eternal life. —Jn 5:24

AUG.
3

The promise of life eternal

REFLECTION. When Jesus speaks of possessing eternal life it is not only a future event. In Catholic theology we refer to the study of end times as eschatology. Jesus slightly shifts our attention and speaks of possessing eternal life now, in the present.

For those who accept Jesus and believe in His words the joy of life eternal begins now!

PRAYER. *Lord Jesus, increase my desire for Your word. Thank You for Your promises.*

DO not accept the praise of men. —Jn 5:41 **AUG. 4**

Flattery will get you nowhere

REFLECTION. Jesus was no fool when it came to those who used empty words to try to influence Him.

Like Jesus, we should desire the praise of God. God is the rightful judge of our hearts and actions and when we play the game of seeking the praise of men rather than God we get off track. May we seek to praise God in all ways.

PRAYER. *Jesus, free me from the desire to be praised by others rather than You.*

HERE is a boy here who has five barley loaves and two fish.

—Jn 6:9 **AUG. 5**

A little is enough in the right hands

REFLECTION. The miraculous act of Jesus in feeding the 5,000 was initiated by Andrew by bringing to Christ a boy who had some loaves and fish. While the disciples looked at the miniscule amount and balked, in Jesus' hands it was enough.

As men of faith it's amazing what we can do with just a little when we unite it to Jesus. Include Him in all of your endeavors.

PRAYER. *Lord God, help me to be generous with whatever gifts I have.*

BUT he said to them, "It is I. Do not be afraid!"

AUG.
—Jn 6:20

6

From fear to faith

REFLECTION. It's not every day that you see someone walking on the water so perhaps the disciples are justified in being afraid. What seems to calm the disciples down is the recognition that it is indeed Jesus who is with them.

Life may throw some strange and frightening situations our way, yet Jesus is present through it all. He says to you; "It is I, do not be afraid!"

PRAYER. *My Lord, comfort me by Your Holy Spirit so I may not be afraid.*

JESUS replied, "This is the work of God: to believe in the one whom he has sent."

AUG.
—Jn 6:29

7

Belief is the work

REFLECTION. To have some quantitative data showing what they have done and a detailed account of their work is important to most men.

The work of God is to believe. For Jesus, belief is not only an intellectual assent to truth but belief is lived out following the words and example of Jesus.

PRAYER. *Heavenly Father, may I never fear to put into practice the words of Your Son.*

MISSION is never the fruit of a perfectly planned program or a well-organized manual. —Pope Francis

God doesn't fit in a box

REFLECTION. Corporations spend much time, energy, and resources on strategic plans to accomplish their goals. God's plan was Jesus. In studying the greatest teacher and evangelist ever we notice that Jesus is open to interruptions; He is prayerful; He gets surprised now and again.

You can't "plan God moments" but you can certainly be open to following His way on mission.

PRAYER. *Holy Spirit, stir within me and make me attentive to Your promptings.*

JESUS answered them, "I am the bread of life." —Jn 6:35

Nourishment for the journey

REFLECTION. As Catholics, we believe in the real presence of Jesus in the Eucharist. This was a difficult teaching for many during the life of Jesus and difficult for some people today. Yet, we are adamant in our belief because it is Jesus who tells us.

This belief has been treasured since the time of the apostles and straight down through their successors today.

PRAYER. *Mary, pray for me that I may worthily receive your Son in the Eucharist.*

YOU fell? Rise up! —Pope Francis **AUG. 10**

No shame in falling

REFLECTION. The path of following Jesus will mean that we will fall multiple times on the journey. We recall that three times Jesus Himself fell while carrying the Cross.

Pope Francis, during a weekday Mass reflected, "You fell? Rise up!" We all fall but that provides an opportunity for us to rise up and try again.

PRAYER. *Lord, You know how often I fall, send Your Holy Spirit and others to raise me up.*

FAITH grows when it is lived and shaped by love. That is why our families, our homes, are true domestic churches.

—Pope Francis **AUG. 11**

Faith grows in the home

REFLECTION. The word home appears over thirty times in the Gospels and the word house appears over ninety times. So much of Jesus' healing, teaching, forgiving, and sharing meals takes place in the home.

If Jesus spent so much time in the home how can we do otherwise for it is in the home that faith is more caught than taught.

PRAYER. *My Lord, may I never be ashamed to live and share my faith at home.*

OW can he say, "I have come down from heaven?" —Jn 6:42 **AUG. 12**

Don't "pigeon hole" people

REFLECTION. One of the first questions we ask one another socially is, "Where are you from?" Our answer may be a state, country, or parish.

Often people make assumptions if they know where we are from. The religious leadership tried to do this with Jesus. They thought they knew where Jesus was from. Our answer is like His; we are all from the heart of the Father.

PRAYER. *Father, remind me that I came from You and I'm a beloved son.*

 N ADULT faith does not follow the waves of fashion and the latest novelties. —Pope Benedict XVI **AUG. 13**

Stay the course

REFLECTION. Every three to five years there seems to be another "paradigm shift" whether it be in business, dieting, or even in models of faith. Pope Benedict XVI reminds us that the man of faith does not get caught up in new trends of belief and novelties in liturgy.

Christ has shown the way and we have the Catechism which lays out what we believe.

PRAYER. *Holy Spirit, the Paraclete, keep me from novelties that draw me away from the Church.*

IF THE Lord does not build the house, those who construct it labor in vain. —Ps 127:1

AUG. 14

A solid foundation

REFLECTION. Prayer should precede and permeate all of our preparation in whatever we do. Marriage, family life, work . . . whatever we are committed to, the Lord should be our foundation.

How often have you modeled your dependence on God with your family or friends? Do you rely on yourself alone or is God in the mix?

PRAYER. *Jesus the Good Shepherd, may I talk to You before undergoing any task.*

BEHOLD, children are a gift from the Lord, a reward of the fruit of the womb. —Ps 127:3

AUG. 15

The gifts of children

REFLECTION. One of the greatest blessings a father can experience is the birth of a child. The first moments when you hold the child in your arms can't be described by words but the experience lasts a lifetime.

A parent soon realizes that the child will become independent and is destined to go out on their own. Treasure each day for a child is truly a gift from God.

PRAYER. *Father of mercies, guide me to be the father and husband You call me to be.*

UT of the depths I cry to you, O Lord; O Lord, hear my voice. —Ps 130:1-2

AUG.
16

Recourse to prayer

REFLECTION. King David, the man of God who was anointed King of Israel, knew how to pray in good times and in bad. Yes, bad! Difficult times come to faithful people and Jesus and King David attest to that fact.

When we are in the depths and close to despair may we lead by example and cry out to God knowing that He is always with us.

PRAYER. *O Lord, hear me when I cry out to You and welcome the prayer that is heartfelt.*

ISRAEL, put your hope in the Lord both now and forevermore —Ps 131:3

AUG.
17

To whom else shall we go?

REFLECTION. God has given everyone a set of natural gifts and talents and we give God glory when we use them according to His will. There are times when we take too much upon ourselves and let our pride get in the way.

We aren't designed to do everything on our own nor does God desire that we suffer through life. Place your hope in the Lord; trust in Him.

PRAYER. *Lord, my hope is in You both now and forever.*

OW wonderful and delightful it is for brothers to live together in unity.

—Ps 133:1

Come together

REFLECTION. We read about division and separation almost every day in the news. Dissension on sports teams and between political parties is commonplace. How wonderful it is to live as brothers in unity of heart and mind.

What are you doing to bring people together and live in unity? Opportunities abound at home and the workplace for sure.

PRAYER. *Holy Trinity, may my family be one as You are one in love and unity.*

RAISE the Lord, for the Lord is good; sing to honor his name, for he is gracious.

—Ps 135:3

Sing to God, really?

REFLECTION. Most Catholic men don't raise their hands in praise of God or sing out His glory to praise Him. However, at a stadium or ball park you can't keep them quiet. Our culture is obsessed with award shows and praises everything from sports stars to musicians to detergent.

Why not begin to praise the God who loves us beyond measure and who saved us?

PRAYER. *Jesus my Lord, may I give You the praise and glory that You deserve each day.*

PUT yourself in God's hands; He abandons no one.

—St. Andre Bessette

Never to leave you

REFLECTION. St. Andre Bessette was the humble doorkeeper at the Oratory of St. Joseph in Montreal. His childlike faith and trust in God led many thousands to both conversion and healing. His advice is that of a doorkeeper: humble and simple.

Each day, when you open the door to leave the house put yourself in God's hands.

PRAYER. *Jesus, may I trust in Your guiding and ever-present hand.*

THERE is no better evidence, no truer proof of a great love of God, than a great love of our neighbor.

—Fr. Thomas A. Judge

To whom are you a neighbor?

REFLECTION. Fr. Thomas A. Judge lived and ministered in the early part of the twentieth century. He understood the great power of faith that the laity possessed and he desired that their faith be shared with others.

How does this happen? It starts by being a neighbor to the ones closest to you—by building friendships and sharing faith with them.

PRAYER. *Lord, help me to be a better neighbor today through my love and service to others.*

THE Lord will fulfill his plan for me.
—Ps 138:8

AUG. 22

We are here with a purpose

REFLECTION. It's always nice to know that somebody is in charge and has a plan. Whether it's a camping trip, vacation, or business, we feel a sense of comfort knowing that someone planned ahead.

While we don't often see the details of the master plan, God's word assures us that His plan for us will be achieved. Move forward joyfully knowing God is in control.

PRAYER. *Lord, help me when I doubt and despair when life seems to go awry.*

LORD, you have examined me and you know me.
—Ps 139:1

AUG. 23

Nothing hidden from God

REFLECTION. Psychologically speaking, it's healthy to have a friend that you can be 100% honest with, where nothing is hidden, and your thoughts and feelings are laid out unashamedly.

Thank God for those men in your life with whom you can share your life with. When those friends are not present remember that with God, you always have an ally that knows you and loves you.

PRAYER. *Holy Spirit, help me to be self-aware even with my faults and failings.*

124

ISTEN, O Lord, to the voice of my supplications

—Ps 140:7

AUG.
24

Our Father listens

REFLECTION. We all have a desire to be heard and listened to. One of life's frustrations is to be ignored and dismissed by others and that experience can make us feel insignificant.

Throughout the Psalms we hear that prayer is a dialogue and that God desires to hear our prayers and supplications. No one is insignificant in the eyes of our Father.

PRAYER. *Lord, I trust in You for all things, may I never hold back my prayers from You.*

OW can a young man lead a spotless life? By living according to your word.

—Ps 119:9

AUG.
25

A way to perfection

REFLECTION. The Bible has often been referred to as a road map to salvation. The average person who picks it up and begins to read it often finds themselves confused with the various names and customs which are foreign to them.

Open to the Gospel of Mark in the New Testament, and begin there. You'll be surprised how the word of God can change your life for the better.

PRAYER. *Jesus, assist me in being disciplined in following Your word.*

OUR word is a lamp for my feet and a light to my path. —Ps 119:105

AUG.
26

Illuminating the way

REFLECTION. Most, if not all, mature Catholic men who are solid in their faith speak of the Bible as one of the ways that their faith is nourished and sustained.

The word of God is alive and active and gives direction to how we should act with Christ as the model. Make room for Jesus by spending time each day reading His word.

PRAYER. *Come Holy Spirit, increase my desire and hunger for God's word.*

O NOT place your trust in princes, in mortal men who have no power to save. —Ps 146:3

AUG.
27

He is the power

REFLECTION. During Jesus' lifetime there was a statue dedicated to Caesar in the hills of Samaria with the inscription: Caesar Augustus: Savior of the World. It was a sign to those who lived in the area that they should place their trust in Rome.

After encountering Jesus they realized that Jesus is the true savior of the world. Trust in Jesus and not in men to save you.

PRAYER. *Lord, may my example of trusting in You inspire other men to do the same.*

EE everything, overlook a great deal, correct a little. —Pope St. John XXIII

AUG. 28

Some papal advice

REFLECTION. Pope St. John XXIII was known for his good sense of humor and his ability to persuade people rather than to "mandate" policy. When one considers that he was responsible for the universal Church his advice speaks both of his wisdom and his trust in others.

How do you like to be managed by others? How do you correct others in your care? Is it Christ-like?

PRAYER. *Lord, let me treat others as I myself like to be treated and managed.*

 ODERN man listens more willingly to witnesses than to teachers, and if he does listen to teachers, it is because they are witnesses.

AUG. 29

—Blessed Paul VI

Be a witness and your words will have power

REFLECTION. Pope Paul VI was on to something when he was writing about evangelization and the power of personal witness.

What do you witness to each day? Are your actions in line with what you believe and profess as a Catholic?

PRAYER. *Jesus the Good Shepherd, may my actions and words reflect that of a man of faith.*

FOR whatever the Father does, the Son also does. **AUG. 30** —Jn 5:19

Like Father like Son

REFLECTION. How true the statement that says we "replicate ourselves in our children." Not only our physical characteristics but our expressions and choice of words are often picked up by our children.

What kind of example have we received from our parents and how can we, as men of God, pass on the best of who we are to our children?

PRAYER. *Our Father, may my example be rooted in my relationship with Jesus.*

I TRUST you, you used me, now my heart's all torn apart. **AUG. 31** —Paul D. Hudson

Trust issues

REFLECTION. There are hundreds if not thousands of songs which speak of broken hearts and misplaced trust. It can be difficult to trust God when the people we love and who say they love us betray our trust.

Those wounds should be offered up to God, and in time we will know healing. What have you learned from the times you betrayed another's trust?

PRAYER. *Lord God, help to restore my trust in others and grow in my trust in You.*

PETER, an apostle of Jesus Christ.

—1 Pet 1:1

SEPT.
1

One who is sent

REFLECTION. When we think of the men that Jesus chose for mission St. Peter is usually the first to come to mind. He's listed first among the apostles and as the spokesperson for them after the descent of the Holy Spirit.

The word apostle literally means "one who is sent." As Peter was sent so are all who are baptized in Christ.

PRAYER. *St. Peter, pray that I may discover and accomplish the mission God has for me.*

FOR you are achieving the goal of your faith, that is, the salvation of your souls.

—1 Pet 1:9

SEPT.
2

Eyes on the prize

REFLECTION. How much time do you spend contemplating Heaven? Most men are focused on the here and now and rarely take the time to think of the afterlife.

True, we have work to do here and now that can help get us to Heaven, but it's good to take some time to look at the big picture every once in a while.

PRAYER. *Holy Trinity, remind me of my ultimate goal which is Heaven.*

 **REPARE your minds for action.**

—1 Pet 1:13

Activity or accomplishment?

REFLECTION. St. Peter is addressing men who have experienced the risen Christ and are now going out to live their faith in a world which is hostile to Christianity. Peter's advice is: "Prepare your minds for action."

There is nothing new about athletes preparing themselves "pre-game" for the contest and visualizing success. Are you mentally prepared to serve Jesus in the world?

PRAYER. *Jesus, may my focus be on the present moment and serving You in those I meet.*

 ND Moses did as the Lord had commanded him.

—Lev 16:34

Trust and obey

REFLECTION. It can be confusing to read some of the books in the Old Testament because of the rituals and regulations. Yet, we read the phrase, "Moses did as the Lord commanded him," several times.

While our minds may desire understanding it seems that obedience is more highly treasured. We are all called to trust and obey God's word.

PRAYER. *Almighty Father, help me to trust in Your word at all times.*

THE Lord answered Moses: Is this beyond the Lord's reach? —Num 11:23

God sees the whole picture

REFLECTION. The trust that a child has in their father replicates the trust that we are called to have in God, our Father. At times the situation appears hopeless and human logic fails to find a solution. Such is the case throughout scripture.

However, in God's hands problems are nothing less than opportunities for God to show us that He loves us and is in control.

PRAYER. *Lord God, reassure me that You indeed are in control.*

DO NOT fear them, for it is the Lord, your God, who will fight for you.
—Deut 3:22

A mighty warrior

REFLECTION. Knowing that you are not alone in any battle or ordeal is a source of great comfort. While we can be that source of strength and comfort for others and others for us, God stands before us as well, fighting for us.

Who and what may God be calling you to fight for? What resources do you have that might be of aid and comfort to another?

PRAYER. *Come Holy Spirit, my Advocate, assist me in fighting for others.*

A S I was with Moses, I will be with you: I will not leave you or forsake you. —Jos 1:5

7

He will stand by you

REFLECTION. Joshua was the man who guided the people into the Promised Land at God's command. He picked up where Moses had left off and commanded the Israelites as they entered it.

These two men shared a trust in God and a close relationship with the Lord. How can you strengthen your trust in and relationship with the Lord?

PRAYER. *Saving Lord, be with me and help me to strengthen my relationship with You each day.*

D O NOT swerve from it either to the right or to the left, that you may succeed wherever you go. — Jos 1:7

SEPT.

8

Keep the law of the Lord

REFLECTION. Men tend to throw away the directions when opening something that needs to be assembled. In some cases they can figure it out while in other cases they need to rummage through the garbage to retrieve them.

God's word is clear if we desire success. No cutting corners and no shortcuts for the man of faith. Grab your Bible; read and apply it.

PRAYER. *Lord God, may I always be attentive to Your word and follow it.*

D O NOT let this book of the law depart from your lips. Recite it by day and by night. —Jos 1:8

SEPT. 9

Memorize the scriptures

REFLECTION. Memorizing the scriptures may seem a little extreme to most Catholics. Think for a moment of all the songs, addresses, and pass codes that you have memorized over the years. Memorization isn't the issue but discipline is.

Athletes must memorize their playbooks in order to function at a high level. Ask God for the grace to commit to memorizing a verse a week.

PRAYER. *Lord, give me a hunger for Your word so I may memorize a portion each week.*

COMMAND you: be strong and steadfast! —Jos 1:9

SEPT. 10

Fear is not an option

REFLECTION. Books on leadership are constantly on the bestsellers' list because leading others effectively can mean a promotion. Some skills can be acquired through study while other skills emerge naturally.

Without the Lord at the center of your life, other leadership qualities will fail in the long term to meet the challenges in your business, personal, and spiritual endeavors.

PRAYER. *Jesus, whatever I do may I begin and end my day with You leading me.*

IN THE future, these are to be a sign among you. —Jos 4:6

Remembering God's goodness

REFLECTION. God commanded Joshua to choose twelve men to each take a stone and place the stone by the banks of the Jordan River where the river ceased to flow when the Ark of the Covenant was present.

We all need reminders of the Lord's presence in our life and to mark them for ourselves and for our children. What God-signs do you share with your family?

PRAYER. *Lord, forgive me for those times I have failed to share Your presence in my life.*

THE Lord then said to Joshua: Do not be afraid or dismayed. —Jos 8:1

All in God's timing

REFLECTION. Joshua, who was the Lord's servant and who witnessed miracles was at times afraid and dismayed. It is part of the human experience and we have all experienced the ups and downs that life can bring.

Being faithful does not make one immune to life's difficulties and complexities. Where is your faith in times of trial?

PRAYER. *O Lord, assure me of Your presence when life doesn't make sense.*

Y LORD," Gideon said to him, "if the Lord is with us, why has all this happened to us?" —Jdg 6:13

SEPT.
13

God raises up saints

REFLECTION. The question asked by Gideon is one that has been asked countless times of how a good and loving God can allow suffering.

The mystery of the Cross provides guidance for Catholics. God can bring about more good from evil than if evil never existed.

PRAYER. *Holy Lord, I trust in You and will remain faithful throughout any trial with Your help.*

"I WILL do whatever you say," Ruth replied. —Ru 3:5

SEPT.
14

Inspiration from afar

REFLECTION. God certainly works within the structures and events that He sets up. Having a routine and regular pattern of action provides a sense of comfort. God is not bound by these structures however.

Every now and again God uses someone from outside the community to reveal what authentic faith looks like. Ruth, a Moabite, was one such example.

PRAYER. *Lord, may I be an inspiration to others because of my unfailing trust in You.*

135

ARLY the next morning they worshiped before the Lord. —1 Sam 1:19

Together before the Lord

REFLECTION. Elkanah and his wife Hannah worshiped together before the Lord. What a gift it is to worship the Lord with the one we love.

Hannah was a woman who was not afraid to pour her heart out to the Lord, and before she received an answer from God we read that they were worshiping God. A couple who trusts in the Lord together make a powerful team.

PRAYER. *My God, thank You for those whom I can worship You with in faith and love.*

AMUEL was displeased when they said, "Give us a king to rule us." —1 Sam 8:6

Be careful what you ask for

REFLECTION. The people wanted to be like other nations and have a king rule over them instead of the Lord. The people got what they asked for.

Kings tax, rule arbitrarily, and send young men to battle. When God is out of the equation disaster usually follows close behind. Catholics are called to stand out from the culture because Jesus is our Lord.

PRAYER. *Lord, may I desire to be like Jesus and not like powerful men of weak faith.*

OD does not see as a mortal, who sees the appearance. The Lord looks into the heart. —1 Sam 16:7

Look within

REFLECTION. How easily are we fooled by people's outward appearance? The sports car, the rings, and finely tailored clothes all can lead us to give the wealthy more respect than others.

Are you like other men who may judge by these outward signs? Pray that you may give all people the respect that they deserve because we are all children of God.

PRAYER. *Jesus, help me to see the heart of others and not be so fast to judge.*

 ITH his sling in hand, he approached the Philistine. —1 Sam 17:40

Slay your Goliath

REFLECTION. The story of David and Goliath is one of the most famous in the Old Testament. David approached with more than just a sling and a stone, however, for he approached and announced the deliverance of Goliath by the power of the Lord.

How do you approach evil and injustice? Are you timid or bold knowing that a man of God fights for justice?

PRAYER. *Holy Spirit, Advocate, may my voice never be silenced in the face of injustice.*

T HE Lord shall be between you and me, **SEPT.** and between your offspring and mine **19** forever. —1 Sam 20:42

A bond between brothers

REFLECTION. King David and Jonathan had a relationship like many who fight in battles together. They stood side by side like police officers, fire fighters, EMS workers and those in the military.

When you find a friend who will fight side by side with you and for you, you have a great gift from God who also stands with us. Who are you thankful for in your life?

PRAYER. *Jesus, thank You for the friends You have given me in my life.*

T HE Lord sent Nathan to David. **SEPT.** —2 Sam 12:1 **20**

A true "gift"

REFLECTION. The Lord sent Nathan to King David. The name Nathan literally means "gift."

What Nathan delivered was a parable in which he asked David to decide how a certain man would be dealt with. In anger, David gave his verdict and Nathan replied, "You are the man!" Nathan was a gift because he could speak honestly with the king who had sinned.

PRAYER. *Jesus, may Your word and the honest words of others correct me when I am wrong.*

HEN David said to Nathan, "I have sinned against the Lord."

—2 Sam 12:13

SEPT.
21

Message received

REFLECTION. One of the greatest attributes of any man is the humility to admit when he is wrong. Sometimes we may be forced to deal with the truth of our sin like David when someone calls us out on it.

Regardless of how our sin is exposed, a good Christian admits his sin and repents. As they say, it takes a big man to admit when he is wrong.

PRAYER. *Lord Jesus, forgive me and provide me with the grace to make amends.*

HEY saw that the king had in him the wisdom of God for giving right judgment.

—1 Ki 3:28

SEPT.
22

The Wisdom of Solomon

REFLECTION. As men get older we expect to gain in wisdom and judgment due to the breadth of our experience. No doubt a certain degree of wisdom comes with age.

Scripture clearly points out that the crowd saw the wisdom of God in Solomon and not just the wisdom that comes with age. True wisdom still comes from God. Ask and you will receive.

PRAYER. *Lord, grant me Your wisdom so my decisions may glorify You.*

LATER Elisha asked, "What can we do for her?"
—2 Ki 4:14

A great question

REFLECTION. Some questions never go out of style. Whether it was 2500 years ago or today asking the simple question, "What can I do for you?" is always in season.

As a Catholic man, it reveals that we, like Christ, have a heartfelt desire to use our gifts for the service of others. Jesus used His gifts to serve and so should we.

PRAYER. *Jesus, may I put myself at the service of others as You did.*

HEZEKIAH held fast to the Lord and never turned away from following him.
—2 Ki 18:6

What will you be remembered for?

REFLECTION. In business there is a phrase which speaks about a man's journey of success. He should learn, earn, and return.

These three ideas are spoken of by top business leaders and the last one, return, reflects the legacy a man leaves behind. For some it may be money and philanthropy and for others perhaps their time and wisdom. What will you return?

PRAYER. *Abba, Father, may I return each day something of the goodness I have received from You.*

FOR everything is from you, and what we give is what we have from you.

—1 Chr 29:14

Everything is a gift on loan

REFLECTION. When we realize that everything we have is a gift from God it will seem only natural to use these gifts to serve Him in some way.

When pride enters in and tells us the lie that everything we have is a result of my own labor and effort we tend to close ourselves off to God and others. How do you view the opportunities and natural gifts you have?

PRAYER. *Blessed Mother Mary, give me your humble heart which gave all praise to God.*

THEY restored the house of God according to its original form, and reinforced it.

—2 Chr 24:13

Proper place of worship

REFLECTION. The men of Israel gathered together to rebuild the Temple and to restore it. It was the central place of worship and had fallen into ruin.

In God's wisdom, He knows that we need to place our focus on Him otherwise our fallen human nature will begin again to place ourselves at the center of our lives. How are you rebuilding the Church?

PRAYER. *Lord Jesus, may I build the Church by building up others in faith.*

ZRA had set his heart on the study and practice of the law of the Lord. —Ezr 7:10

A man of God and an example for all

REFLECTION. Ezra was a priest, scribe, and man who initiated the rebuilding of the altar in the Temple. While in captivity he secured passage from the king to go home and rebuild. The king agreed because he knew that the hand of the Lord was upon Ezra.

When have you exhibited such boldness in something connected with faith?

PRAYER. *Jesus, may we learn from You to correct with gentleness and compassion.*

OME, let us rebuild the wall of Jerusalem, so that we may no longer be a reproach! —Neh 2:17

What and who do you protect?

REFLECTION. Ezra restored the proper place of worship and Nehemiah was tasked with the rebuilding of the wall for protection.

Fathers are constantly protecting their children, spouse, and extended family from physical danger and from offensive shows and images on TV and the computer that injure the mind and soul. We need to take some time to repair any walls in our faith life that may be crumbling.

PRAYER. *My God, guide me in protecting my loved ones from whatever dangers there are.*

142

UT I alone used to go often to Jerusalem for the festivals, as prescribed for all of Israel.

—Tob 1:6

Strength to go it alone

REFLECTION. Cheering on our favorite neighborhood teams and supporting community events are great experiences. A lively and vibrant worship community can make us feel connected to God and others as well.

Are you willing to be like Tobit and go it alone for the sake of God? Tobit was faithful in his obedience to God despite going it alone.

PRAYER. *Jesus the Good Shepherd, assist me in being strong in faith when others are not.*

 HAT happened to you? You're not the same?

—Ian MacKaye

Change can be a good thing

REFLECTION. How often have you said to someone, "Never change!" No doubt these words are said as a compliment because of the wonderful qualities we see in the other person.

But change is constant and indeed good. Our growth as a person and more importantly our growth as a beloved son of God will demand that we change and conform to the person of Jesus.

PRAYER. *Lord God, may I never see change as a threat but as an invitation to grow.*

LL the men of Israel cried to God with great fervor and humbled themselves.
—Jud 4:9

We are in this together

REFLECTION. When a crisis struck Israel the book of Judith recounts the actions of the men who cried out to God. They recognized that their strength lie in their relationship with God.

What a wonderful model for men today. Too often we try to go it alone when there are others who are experiencing the same crisis. Who has supported you in prayer and how can you support others?

PRAYER. *Lord, remind me that my strength lies in my relationship with You.*

ECALLING all that the Lord had done, Mordecai prayed to the Lord. —Est C:1

A model to follow

REFLECTION. Fathers know that their children's behavior is more caught than taught. That is, children watch and absorb more through behavior than what they hear from adults.

Mordecai provides a wonderful example of what a man of God does when there is a crisis: he prays. God knows what God has done, but Mordecai recalls it for reassurance.

PRAYER. *Jesus my Savior, may my prayer be an example for my children.*

CHILDREN! Be courageous and strong in keeping the law, for by it you shall be honored. —1 Mac 2:64

Strength and honor

REFLECTION. The book of Maccabees is one of the bloodiest books in the Old Testament. In it we find Judas Maccabee, a strong leader and defender of Israel and the laws of God, who stands firm in resisting those who would betray God be they Jews or Gentiles.

Fidelity to the law was an expression of the love of God. Have you ever defended the faith?

PRAYER. *Lord, may my faith stand the test of opposition in the face of those who don't believe.*

IT IS, in fact, a sign of great kindness to punish the impious promptly instead of letting them go for long. —2 Mac 6:13

Punishment as kindness?

REFLECTION. Young people often don't recognize the kindness shown by teachers, parents, and coaches who punish bad behavior. Adults know that letting the bad behavior continue will only result in trouble down the road.

God corrects and punishes for the same reason. As children trust in the guidance of their parents we too should trust in God's wisdom and correction.

PRAYER. *My God, may I receive correction with understanding when I have been unjust.*

145

O YOU give the horse his strength, and clothe his neck with a mane?
—Job 39:19

Who is in control?

REFLECTION. The book of Job is perhaps the oldest book in the Old Testament and its main character, Job, is well known for his suffering. God responds because He respects Job, yet God's response is strange for he asks a number of questions which are unanswerable.

In the end God wants to teach Job that God knows and God is in control. Like Job, we are called to trust.

PRAYER. *Mary, Mother of God, help me to trust God the Father in all things.*

HERE is an appointed time for everything, and a time for every affair under the heavens.
—Eccl 3:1

Turn, turn, turn

REFLECTION. In the late 1960s a band turned the words of Ecclesiastes into a hit song. We live out the appointed time for planting, weeping, and so on at every age and every stage of our lives.

There is no need to become anxious as a man of God because we know that God is already there at every age and every stage of our lives.

PRAYER. *Jesus, thank You for always being present in my life.*

ET me as a seal upon your heart, as a seal upon your arm; For Love is as strong as Death. —Song 8:6

7

You are mine

REFLECTION. The Book of the Song of Songs is unique in many ways. There is no mention of God, Jerusalem, prayer, the law and many other elements we would expect in a book of scripture. Yet love is the focus.

The attraction between a man and a woman is played out in all its splendor. Where there is love, God is in the mix.

PRAYER. *Loving Lord, thank You for those who have loved me and continue to love me.*

OR the first step toward Wisdom is an earnest desire for discipline. —Wis 6:17

OCT.

8

Put one foot in front of the other

REFLECTION. Wisdom does not seem to be valued much these days. In an age where people desire instant gratification and where moral relativism reigns wisdom gets discounted.

God's word is clear however that wisdom is to be desired and it is connected to loving God's word. In an age where people desire things, pray for wisdom and read His word.

PRAYER. *Come Holy Spirit, give me a hunger and yearning for scripture.*

147

Y CHILD, when you come to serve the Lord, prepare yourself for trials.

OCT. 9

—Sir 2:1

Not an easy road

REFLECTION. Late night commercials for exercise equipment and programs are usually prefaced by how "easy" it is to get in shape or acquire "abs of steel." Most men turn the channel because they know it's a lie.

Anything that's worth doing involves a degree of difficulty, sacrifice, and discipline. Following the Lord brings joy but remember, we too must carry a cross.

PRAYER. *Lord, save me from prosperity Christianity which is devoid of the Cross.*

 HE optimist says, "I can do it," the pessimist says, "I can't do it," and the realist does it.

OCT. 10

—Brian Honsberger

Get real!

REFLECTION. At times, people who become serious about their faith, replace action with discernment. Discerning God's will is good, but perpetual discernment is not.

Believing is faith in action and our model, Jesus, was an example of this. In what areas of your life do you need to put your faith into action? Discern and then act.

PRAYER. *Merciful Lord, may I never stop acting because I'm afraid of making a mistake.*

OMFORT, give comfort to my people, says your God. —Isa 40:1

The strong give comfort

REFLECTION. We think that before a person can give comfort they must know that someone is in need of comforting. However, there are times when our children or other family members are comforted just by knowing we are present.

The presence of a significant person in our lives can mean the difference between comfort and despair. Give comfort by being present even in difficult circumstances.

PRAYER. *Lord God, may the comfort of Your presence in my life help me to be present for others.*

———————

REMEMBER the devotion of your youth. —Jer 2:2

OCT.

12

Where are you today?

REFLECTION. Serving the Lord as an altar boy or being involved in high school ministry is fine, but has your devotion stopped there?

The Lord remembers the devotion we have had toward Him, but He wants us to grow closer to Him so that we may enjoy His abundant love.

PRAYER. *Jesus, may my devotion be ongoing and more intense as the years go by.*

149

T IS good to hope in silence for the Lord's deliverance.   —Lam 3:26

Waiting is the hardest part

REFLECTION. It's becoming much more difficult to wait, to be patient in our society. The gift of the information age and technology is that information can be accessed at the speed of light.

God does not operate on our timetable so therefore we wait. We don't wait in vain but as the author of Lamentations states, in "hope." How difficult is it for you to hope in silence?

PRAYER. *Mary, Mother of God, pray for me to hope in all circumstances for God's deliverance.*

EAR, Israel, the commandments of life: listen, and know prudence!   —Bar 3:9

Right reason in action

REFLECTION. "Hear." "Listen." These words are repeated throughout scripture so God is trying to get our attention it seems.

How often are we distracted in our pursuit of God? We may have good intentions but "life happens," and we find ourselves away from the Lord. Prudence is "right reason in action," so listening to the Word of God and putting it in practice leads to life.

PRAYER. *Heavenly Father, slow me down that I may not miss out on the life You have prepared for me.*

THEIR children are bold of face and stubborn of heart—to them I am sending you.

—Ezek 2:4

Send me!

REFLECTION. The Navy Seals are considered one of the most selective outfits in the military. Those who earn the title of Navy Seal go through intense training and challenges that only one in hundreds can complete. No extra pay. No fancy perks. Extremely dangerous missions lie ahead.

To bring generations to the Lord is a challenge. Will you do it?

PRAYER. *Lord, I don't see myself as a missionary: adjust my vision to see others as You do.*

THEY walked about in the flames, singing to God and blessing the Lord.

—Dan 3:24

A burning ring of fire

REFLECTION. The story of Daniel and his three friends in the fiery furnace is one of the most popular stories in the Old Testament. What got them in the fire was faith. They made a conscious decision to follow the way of the Lord and not bow down to the king.

What principles and beliefs will you stand up for despite the cost?

PRAYER. *Lord, increase my courage so I may take a stand for You and for the dignity of life.*

Y PEOPLE are ruined for the lack of knowledge! —Hos 4:6

Catechesis is a must

REFLECTION. Hosea lived in a time of great infidelity. We can look around and say the same thing about Catholics in our culture today. Eighty-seven percent of Catholic young adults who are baptized and confirmed no longer practice the faith.

We can shake our heads about this statistic or we can do something about it. Are you increasing your knowledge of the faith and sharing it with others?

PRAYER. *St. Michael the Archangel, pray for us to teach and defend the faith.*

 T SHALL come to pass I will pour out my spirit upon all flesh. —Joel 3:1

We are all chosen people

REFLECTION. When there is a crisis what God tends to do is to raise up saints. Throughout the scriptures when the people abandoned God, He responded not with earthquakes and thunder but with people.

God's Holy Spirit is available to you and me. The same Holy Spirit that was in Christ Jesus is available to you!

PRAYER. *Holy Spirit, Advocate, stir within me to make me the man of God You desire.*

ET justice surge like waters, and righteousness like an unfailing stream.
—Am 5:24

OCT.
19

A passion for justice

REFLECTION. Martin Luther King Jr. famously quoted this passage from the prophet Amos in his "I Have a Dream" speech. God is warning us that songs of praise are useless if actions of justice and mercy don't accompany them.

Surging waters are unstoppable as the footage of many natural disasters show. Men who are righteous and stand up for justice are equally unstoppable.

PRAYER. *Abba Father, may my praise be accompanied by righteousness and action.*

ONAH made ready to flee Tarshish, away from the Lord.
—Jon 1:3

OCT.
20

The choices we face

REFLECTION. Jonah was a believer in the Lord. He knew God's voice and heard it. Jonah thought that the Lord was only able to operate in the region of Israel and therefore he fled. God brought him back.

Knowing the Lord and being attuned to His voice are good things, but obeying God is what counts. Even when what God asks is difficult the man of God obeys and doesn't flee.

PRAYER. *Merciful God, forgive me for those times I have failed to carry out Your will.*

NLY to do justice and to love goodness, and to walk humbly with your
God. —Mic 6:8

The requirements are few

REFLECTION. In sports the mantra is often "the main thing is the main thing." This is a way of saying that if your job is to play defense in basketball, well, play defense! Don't get caught up in all the other distractions on the court and outside the game.

The Lord reminds us as He did to the people in the prophet Micah's day that the main thing is the main thing.

PRAYER. *Good Shepherd, lead me back to the basics of my faith so to walk closer to You.*

WILL stand at my guard post, and station
myself upon the rampart. —Hab 2:1

Ready position

REFLECTION. Most people are familiar with military language and images. Here the prophet paints a picture of himself like a soldier ready for battle, in ready position.

For the Catholic man the ready position is falling down upon one's knees in prayer, ready to listen to the direction and prompting of the Holy Spirit. His training manual is the Bible. Are you in ready position?

PRAYER. *Lord, I am ready and attentive. Use me to bring the light of the Gospel to others.*

O NOT fear, Zion, do not be discour-
aged!
—Zep 3:16

We are a people of hope

REFLECTION. Time and time again we read these words in scripture calling us to trust and fear not. God our Father repeats these words over and over because He obviously knows our tendency towards doubt and despair.

As God comforts us we are called to comfort one another. Often our presence is enough but like God, words are sometimes necessary to rouse the spirit and provide encouragement.

PRAYER. *Jesus, open my eyes and mouth so I may encourage another person today.*

HUS says the Lord of hosts: Reflect on
your experience!
—Hag 1:7

Reflection and action

REFLECTION. The Lord uses this expression twice within a few verses of the Old Testament Book of Haggai. How often do we move forward without reflecting or taking time to process events?

The Examen prayer of St. Ignatius asks the one who prays to reflect upon the day to see where joy was experienced. Over time a pattern emerges. What has your experience revealed about God?

PRAYER. *Jesus, when I'm harsh with others, let me reflect on Your treatment of me.*

O NOT oppress the widow or the orphan, the resident alien or the poor.

OCT. 25

—Zec 7:10

Social security

REFLECTION. God's commands always have an eye out for the downtrodden. Rarely do we use the term "widows and orphans" today but our society will always have those who are left on the margins.

If you wish to get God angry then oppress or ignore the poor and vulnerable of our society. Catholic men are called to be the defenders of the weak and the poor. It's who we are.

PRAYER. *Just Lord, may I never oppress the poor with my words or by my actions.*

 OW I am sending my messenger—he will prepare the way before me.

OCT. 26

—Mal 3:1

Whom shall I send?

REFLECTION. The last Book of the Old Testament looks forward to the fulfillment of the promised messiah. Catholics are familiar with John the Baptist who "prepared the way" for the Lord in the desert.

As Catholic men the best legacy we can leave behind is the legacy of faith for it's the only thing that has eternal effects. Will you leave a legacy of faith?

PRAYER. *Come Holy Spirit, here I am, use me to share the Good News of Jesus with others.*

EARS from now, what will your family remember about you?

—Louis Beauregard

Faith, Hope, and Love

REFLECTION. A family has a real treasure if they possess photographs of great grandparents and other relatives going back one hundred years or more. Many websites can help you find your ancestors and build your family tree.

While these faces and stories are intriguing, do we really ever get the whole picture of who they are? How prominent will your faith be when your story is shared?

PRAYER. *God Almighty, may I pass my faith on through my words and example.*

 O NOT let what you cannot do interfere with what you can do.

—John Wooden

Go with your strength

REFLECTION. Coach John Wooden was a man of faith as well as a legendary basketball coach. He knew that character mattered and he knew how to get the best out of his team. His wisdom here fits for both the athlete and disciple of Jesus.

The Lord has given us both natural gifts and spiritual gifts. Using the gifts we have will enable us to maximize our potential. Focusing on what we don't have leads to despair.

PRAYER. *Lord, You know me and my gifts. Help me use them to serve You and others.*

E'LL win tonight. —Mark Messier **OCT. 29**

A bold prediction that will last a lifetime

REFLECTION. Many athletes make bold predictions but few can make them stick. Hockey player Mark Messier not only guaranteed success in game six of a Stanley Cup playoff game, he scored three goals to solidify game seven which his team won.

His boldness makes me think of my confidence in both God and the abilities He has given me. Is your faith in Jesus as bold as Messier's confidence in winning?

PRAYER. *God Almighty, instill in me a bold and confident faith in Your Son Jesus.*

 GNORANCE of scripture is ignorance of Christ. —St. Jerome **OCT. 30**

The Word is alive and active

REFLECTION. St. Jerome is the patron saint of scripture scholars. His words are as true today as they were when he first spoke them. Sometimes hearing the Word at Mass is like receiving a puzzle piece without seeing the whole picture.

It takes two minutes and thirty eight seconds to read an average chapter of the Gospels. Don't be ignorant!

PRAYER. *Lord, increase my desire for You through coming to know You in Your Word.*

O YOU'VE been to school for a year or two and you think you've seen it all.
—J. Biafra

OCT.
31

With age comes wisdom

REFLECTION. Young people's excitement at new adventures brings an attentive ear from family and friends. While their adventures are new for them with age does come a little wisdom.

What wisdom have you gleaned over the years that your faith has taught you? Do you have any lessons for the younger generation?

PRAYER. *Merciful Lord, allow me to share my wisdom with a younger person and help me lead them to You.*

 ESUS stopped and called them, saying, "What do you want me to do for you?"
—Mt 20:32

NOV.
1

Called to serve

REFLECTION. Jesus encounters two blind men in Jericho and asks them a question. Jesus knew they were blind but asked the question anyway perhaps to allow them to articulate their need. Before Jesus asked the question however, He stopped.

The Lord stopped. How often do we stop and notice the people around us whom we may be able to help? As Jesus served so must we.

PRAYER. *Jesus Christ, may Your agenda for the day be my agenda.*

E OVERTURNED the tables of the money changers and the seats of those who were selling doves. —Mt 21:12

Righteous anger

REFLECTION. Few scenes in the Gospels are more shocking than when Jesus turns over the tables and causes a great disturbance in the temple area.

What makes you angry? Perhaps when we meet Jesus in heaven He will ask us why we weren't angrier about injustice, poverty, discrimination, and blasphemy. With the mind of Christ we know what should anger us.

PRAYER. *Jesus, may my response to injustice be a catalyst for positive change.*

HATEVER you ask for in faith-filled prayer, you will receive. —Mt 21:22

Unwavering faith

REFLECTION. There is a healthy tension between faith and answered prayers. God is a loving Father and would not allow our prayers to be answered if they harmed us or our salvation. What Jesus exhibits to the disciples through the cursing of the fig tree is an unwavering faith.

Is prayer your steering wheel or your spare tire? Men of God lead with prayer and then trust in God.

PRAYER. *Heavenly Father, may my prayer be filled with faith in You!*

YOU are in error because you do not understand the scriptures or the power of God. —Mt 22:29

Don't be ignorant

REFLECTION. Jesus is certainly open to questions and throughout the Gospels He entertains questions from many types of people.

We sense some anger in Jesus' response to the religious leaders' questions, however, because their questions are not seeking information but seeking rather to entrap Jesus. When we know scripture and God's power we won't be misled.

PRAYER. *Holy Spirit, reveal to me more deeply the heart of God the Father.*

 WOE to you, scribes and Pharisees, you hypocrites! —Mt 23:23

Admonish the sinner

REFLECTION. One of the spiritual works of mercy is to admonish the sinner. There may be a part of us that desires to point the finger of blame at others who are hypocrites, but then we remember that we are not perfect so we keep quiet.

In Christian love, however, we need not be perfect to admonish someone we love who is in danger of harming themselves or losing their salvation.

PRAYER. *Father, help me to know the words to say when confronting sinful behavior.*

TAY awake, for you know neither the day nor the hour. —Mt 25:13

The end of days

REFLECTION. Every few years we read of someone predicting with certainty that the end of the world is near. It can be alarming and may make us rethink our "readiness."

Jesus is clear in that no one knows the day or hour of His return. For this reason, His advice is important: stay awake. Is your faith in need of a wake-up call? Be prepared spiritually.

PRAYER. *Merciful Lord, may I always be awake, alert, and doing Your will.*

 INCE you have been faithful in small matters, I will give you much greater responsibilities. —Mt 25:21

Promotions available

REFLECTION. In the business world the "newbie" has to prove himself and then, if he has done an exceptional job, he often gets promoted.

Jesus speaks of a similar situation. While we don't earn our salvation, it is a gift; responsibility in matters of faith come to those who are faithful in their discipleship.

PRAYER. *Risen Lord, may faithfulness be my daily goal as I follow You each day.*

IS master said to him, "Well done, my good and faithful servant." —Mt 25:23

NOV. 8

Words of praise

REFLECTION. These words of Jesus are spoken near the end of one of His parables. While we don't refer to workers as "servants," it's easy to make the correlation to today's world.

Whether these words are spoken by a supervisor or coach they are nice words to hear. We especially long to hear those words from God at the end of our lives. Who do you need to speak those words to?

PRAYER. *Eternal Father, may my actions lived in faith merit a "well done" from You.*

 ORD, when did we see you hungry and give you something to eat, or thirsty and give you something to drink? —Mt 25:37

NOV. 9

See Christ in all

REFLECTION. When Jesus speaks of judgment He does not ask if they believe but rather if their beliefs have been put into practice through serving others.

Giving intellectual assent and acknowledging that Jesus is Lord is good and true. Yet it is not enough for the disciple of Christ. Our faith and love need to be put into concrete actions of service and charity.

PRAYER. *Mary, Mother of God, pray for me that my actions would be that of your Son.*

163

THEN one of the Twelve, the man called Judas Iscariot, went to the chief priests. —Mt 26:14

What a name

REFLECTION. There have been people who have made some serious mistakes in sports that are forever remembered for their error and for blowing the big moment. In business, as well, there have been scandals that are forever associated with one name. All pale in comparison to Judas' betrayal.

If you have betrayed Christ by your actions, forgiveness is available. Confess your sin and be free.

PRAYER. *Jesus, may I always find hope and a new beginning in You.*

TAKE this and eat; this is my body. —Mt 26:26

No confusion

REFLECTION. Scripture scholars enjoy finding cultural nuances to the words of Jesus and studying the original language.

Jesus is crystal clear at the Last Supper when speaking about the Eucharist. Jesus didn't change His teaching to please the crowd, and the disciples knew that He meant what He said. He means it at each Mass.

PRAYER. *Eucharistic Lord, I believe that You are truly present in the Eucharist; may I receive You worthily.*

Y FATHER, if it is possible, allow this cup to be taken from me. Yet let your will, not mine, be done. —Mt 26:39

NOV.
12

God's will first

REFLECTION. No one likes to suffer. Jesus, in His agony in the garden, felt the burden of our sin. He had witnessed firsthand the brutality of the Romans and knew what lay ahead for Him.

In the midst of Jesus' anguish, His plea is for God's will to be done. On both our good and not-so-good days may God's will be done.

PRAYER. *Come Holy Spirit, strengthen my resolve to do Your will, whatever the cost.*

 HE life of Jesus is a life for others. It is a life of service. —Pope Francis

NOV.
13

Give it back to God

REFLECTION. Pope Francis is rarely photographed outside the company of others. Many of the photographs are with people who are not even Christian. He reaches out and serves not because of who they are but because of the example of Jesus.

Each day there are opportunities for service. Even those who are homebound can pray, email, and reach out to others with a kind word.

PRAYER. *Lord, may my life mirror Yours in how I serve others.*

NXIETY is the mark of spiritual insecurity.
—Thomas Merton

Whom do we trust?

REFLECTION. Reasons to be worried, upset, or anxious come to all people—atheists and spiritual people alike. Reflection on those anxieties is a good way to measure our spiritual temperature for then we will know what to do with them.

The Christian brings those anxieties to Christ in prayer. Our confidence in God's provision and love will see us through to the end.

PRAYER. *Jesus, when anxiety comes my way may I cast all my cares on You for You care for me.*

 O NOT be fearful. Go and tell my brethren to go to Galilee. There they will see me.
—Mt 28:10

True to His word

REFLECTION. After the Resurrection an angel appears to Mary Magdalene and another woman named Mary and bids them to not be afraid. Jesus Himself, the risen Lord, appears and also tells them not to be afraid.

While fear may be their initial reaction it is not their final reaction. The presence of Jesus is enough to quell their fear. How can your presence bring people assurance?

PRAYER. *Our Father, may my faith and presence lead others to Your Son.*

HE ALONE loves the Creator perfectly who manifests a pure love for his neighbor. —St. Bede the Venerable

NOV.
16

A pure heart create in me

REFLECTION. Purity is not a subject that is popular today, although looking at the current television programing and the covers of magazines at the newsstand perhaps it should be.

Jesus said, "Blessed are the pure in heart for they shall see God." St. Bede makes the natural connection between loving God through loving neighbor. Who will you show God's love to today?

PRAYER. *Jesus our hope, may my thoughts and actions be pure as I serve You and my neighbor.*

ND behold, I am with you always, to the end of the age. —Mt 28:20

NOV.
17

Words of assurance

REFLECTION. The last recorded words of Jesus in Matthew's Gospel are words of assurance. These words shouldn't be separated from the beginning of Jesus' statement however.

He commands disciples to make disciples, baptize, and teach. In doing these things Christ becomes alive in us. He remains present in the Eucharist as well because He loves us so much.

PRAYER. *Jesus, thank You for Your presence and for remaining with us in the Eucharist.*

THE more I practice the luckier I get.

—Gary Player

NOV.
18

Discipline and attention to detail

REFLECTION. Gary Player is a golf legend and like most pros has the ability to make it look easy. While Gary Player and a host of other athletes have natural ability, he makes a good point about practice.

In the spiritual life saints are not made overnight but over a lifetime. Every day we have opportunities to practice our faith, overcome obstacles, and serve others. Practice is key.

PRAYER. *Lord, help me to take advantage of every opportunity to improve my service.*

JUST keep going. Everybody gets better if they keep at it.

—Ted Williams

NOV.
19

Keep your eye on the ball

REFLECTION. The sentiment of the greatest hitter in baseball is to keep on keeping on.

In the spiritual life, if we want to be experts at prayer we need to pray. Spending quiet time with scripture, with formal prayers, and with hearts open to God is the way to perfection. In what area of your spiritual life do you need to be persistent?

PRAYER. *Jesus, let me never give up hope that I can be a saint.*

LESS those who curse you, pray for those who mistreat you.   —Lk 6:28

Are you for real?

REFLECTION. It's no wonder why the early listeners and followers of Jesus never forgot His words for they were so challenging and unintuitive.

Most people naturally desire to curse those who curse them and hurt those who mistreat them. What Jesus asks is not natural but supernatural. Think Christianity is easy? Try living it out!

PRAYER. *Holy Spirit, stir within me to live out the teaching of Jesus with power.*

OU miss 100 percent of the shots you don't take.   —Wayne Gretzky

He shoots, he scores!

REFLECTION. If you want to score in hockey you need to shoot the puck. You don't shoot the puck every time you have it because the opportunity doesn't always present itself.

What are the "shots" that a life of faith calls us to? The shot that serving others is the right thing to do, the shot that reaching out to those on the margins makes a profound difference.

PRAYER. *Lord Jesus, may I be hungry to give this day and the next my best shot.*

O HEALTHY tree can bear rotten fruit, nor does a rotten tree bear healthy fruit. —Lk 6:43

Good roots provide for good fruit

REFLECTION. Jesus was a master at using His surroundings to convey something about the Kingdom of God. Something as ordinary as a tree is used to explain "fruitfulness."

There are a few important elements that help fruit to grow, but the most important is the soil. What or rather who, are your "roots" grounded in? Sink your roots in Christ for a fruitful life.

PRAYER. *Guardian Angel, pray for me so I may bear good fruit that will last.*

 O YOU see this woman? —Lk 7:44

Vision check

REFLECTION. Luke recounts a story of Simon the Pharisee inviting Jesus to dine with him. In the midst of the meal a woman enters and lavishes Jesus with outward signs of respect and love. Simon sees only a sinful woman but Christ sees more.

What is the challenge for us today? How do we view others? We are invited by Jesus to see God's presence within everyone.

PRAYER. *St. Agnes, increase my spiritual vison so I may see the Lord's handiwork in all.*

THOUGH the just fall seven times, they rise again.
—Prov 24:16

NOV.
24

Rise again and again

REFLECTION. In Old Testament terms the word "just" translates as "holy." As men of faith we are well aware of our own weaknesses and missteps as we sincerely try to follow Christ.

When we do fall our response is not to despair but to rise again. We can rise again and again because our life of faith is a journey. The "just" man also helps his brother up when he falls.

PRAYER. *Father God, may I draw inspiration from the saints who fell yet rose to do Your will.*

 RICH and poor have a common bond: the Lord is the maker of them all.
—Prov 22:2

NOV.
25

Know whom you stand before

REFLECTION. Satan is the master of division. We see his activity in the Garden of Eden dividing man and woman from God, and throughout the letters of St. Paul we are warned against divisions.

God in Himself is perfect unity: the Holy Trinity. Catholic men must treat all people with equality and dignity or else our words and prayers will be hypocritical.

PRAYER. *Holy Trinity, may I bring unity where there is division.*

171

HOSOEVER cares for the poor lends to the Lord, who will pay back the sum in full. —Prov 19:17

NOV.
26

See Christ in all

REFLECTION. The author of the Proverbs speaks from the wisdom of the God-fearing community. Consistent with the word of God we find a concern for the poor and those on the margins.

Our faith reveals that God's spirit is alive in every human being. Care for the poor whom God brings your way, and leave the payback to God who won't be outdone in generosity.

PRAYER. *Lord, use me to care for Your poor both materially and spiritually.*

 SOWER went out to sow his seed. —Lk 8:5

NOV.
27

Scattered

REFLECTION. The parable of the sower and the seed is wasteful to American ears. Why would you sow in places you expect no growth? Ah, the power of God to surprise us.

How often do we speak of faith to those people who are not "religious?" How often do we reach out to those who we think will not respond to God?

PRAYER. *Merciful Lord, help me to spread Your word in unexpected places.*

Y MOTHER and my brethern are those who hear the word of God and put it into action. —Lk 8:21

Family redefined

REFLECTION. Our ancestry and genealogy can be exciting to discover. Those famous and ordinary people that are in our family tree explain, in part, our physical features and history.

When it comes to faith however, we can't rely on the faith of our great uncle or mother to save us. In the end, faith is an action we choose every day. Do your actions reflect to others that you've heard God's word?

PRAYER. *Mother of God, thank you for being the first to hear the word of God and act on it.*

 HEN Jesus asked him, "What is your name?" —Lk 8:30

First things first

REFLECTION. As the disciples pull their boat upon the shore in Galilee after a violent storm they are confronted with a crazed, unchained demoniac. While the disciples must have drawn back in shock, Jesus asks the sick man: "What is your name?"

Sharing the faith and building relationships begins with knowing each other's name. Who is God leading you to get to know better?

PRAYER. *Lord, what a joy to know that scripture reveals that You know each one us by name.*

RE you taking over or are you taking orders? Are you going backwards or are you going forwards?

—Joe Strummer

Don't sway with the wind

REFLECTION. It's easy to get caught up in following the crowd. Leaving the decision-making process to others so they can choose for us is often less difficult and time consuming.

The life of faith demands that we decide for Christ. To move forward means that our worldview is that of Christ's. We freely choose to allow Him to take over our lives.

PRAYER. *Almighty God, may the world know and see by my actions that I follow You.*

HEY laughed at him because they knew that she had died. —Lk 8:53

Is God mocked?

REFLECTION. As men of faith we follow the footsteps of Jesus who, at times, was ridiculed and mocked. This did not prevent Jesus from walking in faith and raising a little girl from the dead.

Catholics and their faith are mocked and ridiculed for beliefs that have their roots in scripture and sacred tradition. Stand firm in faith and be the witness to the truth.

PRAYER. *My God, I forget that You were mocked and ridiculed, may I make reparation for those sins of unbelief.*

ET us live today with eyes fixed on the holy will of God. —Blessed M. Celine Borzecka

Fearless and focused

REFLECTION. There is a cacophony of sound when musicians warm up before a concert. Each tuning their instruments making sure that they, individually, are in tune. When they are brought together by the conductor and play from the same songbook the music they make can be heavenly.

When we focus on Jesus and His will and use our gifts, people glimpse heaven.

PRAYER. *Gracious and Loving Lord, may my eyes be fixed on You and Your holy will.*

 E SHOULD be content with this sole satisfaction that by God's grace, we have tried to do as well as we could. —Fr. Thomas A. Judge

Perfection only in Heaven

REFLECTION. God the Father knows our hearts and our desire to serve Him and follow the way of Jesus. At the end of the day, after we have examined how we acted and the choices we made, we should be content that we tried.

Acknowledging our failures and handing them over to divine providence is a good sign that we have not given up. It's His work through us that matters.

PRAYER. *Jesus, I am still running the race of faith, help me to do my best always.*

ANYONE who wishes to follow me must deny himself and take up his cross daily. —Lk 9:23

DEC. 4

Not just on Sunday, every day

REFLECTION. Jesus most likely would not be able to make it in the marketing business today. He plainly tells His would-be followers that following requires one to take up his cross daily and deny himself!

Jesus' way is very different than so many phony preachers who try to sell a "prosperity Gospel." Riches are not guaranteed but heaven awaits.

PRAYER. *Jesus, I am ready and willing with Your Holy Spirit to follow You wherever You lead.*

GO ON your way. Behold, I am sending you out like lambs among wolves. —Lk 10:3

DEC. 5

No easy mission

REFLECTION. How often do we try to make difficult missions or tasks appear easy. Perhaps psychologically it helps us or helps those who are on the fence to take up the mission.

Lambs among wolves? Really! Those who are bringing the message of forgiveness and good news to others have a difficult task. Are you up for the mission?

PRAYER. *Jesus, send me! With Your Holy Spirit I am up for the task.*

HEN the time comes, the Holy Spirit will teach you what you are to say. —Lk 12:12

DEC. 6

Never at a loss for words

REFLECTION. Jesus assures His disciples that when they are engaged in sharing the Good News and defending the faith that the Holy Spirit will come to their aid.

Imagine if each Catholic man was able to articulate his faith with one person each week. The Holy Spirit has the words. Do we step out and speak?

PRAYER. *Come Lord Jesus, speak through me to draw others to You.*

 OU are of far greater importance than birds! —Lk 12:24

DEC. 7

A view from above

REFLECTION. Jesus used comparisons throughout His ministry to reveal our value through the eyes of God. Luke records one of these comparisons where Jesus places people on one hand and birds on the other.

Do our actions and treatment of people reflect what we proclaim about God's love for us?

PRAYER. *Jesus our Lord, use me to reveal to others how valuable they are to me and You.*

177

THE Mother of the Redeemer has a precise place in the plan of salvation.

—Pope St. John Paul II

Behold your Mother

REFLECTION. It is difficult to find a pope or a saint who does not have a devotion to Mary, Mother of the Redeemer. While Marian devotions may seem more appropriate for women, the fact is that Mary is the model disciple for all believers. Her "yes" to God set into motion salvation for all.

How can devotion and study of the Blessed Virgin increase your spiritual life and discipleship?

PRAYER. *Hail Mary, be with me and lead me to your precious and beloved Son.*

FASTEN your belts for service and have your lamps lit.

—Lk 12:35

Ready for action

REFLECTION. For soldiers, "fasten your belt" meant to tie up the long robe you were wearing which makes it easier to move about for battle.

Jesus uses this imagery for His disciples. Men who follow Christ must obey His words and be ready to serve. Are you ready and actively seeking to serve God?

PRAYER. *Jesus, may I be ever ready to serve You and obey Your commands.*

O OUT to the open roads and along the hedgerows and compel people to come so that my house may be filled.

—Lk 14:23

Compel them to come

REFLECTION. In the parable of the Great Feast we read about those who initially accepted the invitation to dine suddenly offering lame excuses and declining to come. The response of the host was to open the doors to all.

This act of grace is still available to you and me. The table is prepared each Sunday and we are all invited.

PRAYER. *Lord, may I never take Your invitation to share in the sacred body and blood of Your Son for granted.*

HE tax collectors and sinners were all crowding around to listen to Jesus.

—Lk 15:1

How do you draw near?

REFLECTION. People draw near to God for a variety of reasons. Some draw near to ask for things, others to thank God for prayers answered or to ask forgiveness.

These are all acceptable ways of praying, but do you ever go to God just to listen? Perhaps we would do better if we spent time each day in silence listening to the Lord.

PRAYER. *My Lord, may I place myself before You each day to listen in the silence of my heart.*

DO NOT fear any illness or vexation, anxiety or pain. Am I not here who am your Mother?

—Mary's words to St. Juan Diego

A mother's care

REFLECTION. The image of Our Lady of Guadalupe is responsible for converting a continent to Christianity. Under an electron microscope you can discern the images of St. Juan Diego and others in the reflection of Mary's eyes.

This is utterly amazing and while even the pigment of the image baffles NASA scientists her message is beautiful: Am I not your Mother?

PRAYER. *Mary, still my soul and allow me to accept your motherly love and care for me.*

AMEN, Amen, I say to you, I am the gate for the sheep. —Jn 10:7

The gatekeeper

REFLECTION. Shepherds would naturally seek places where there is a water source and green grass for the sheep they are entrusted with. When staying overnight with them they would gather scrub brush into a semi-circle next to a hillside to make an enclosure. The shepherd would then lay across the entrance and be the gate.

Jesus, the Good Shepherd, is our protection.

PRAYER. *Lord Jesus, as You lay down Your life for me, may I lay it down for my loved ones.*

HAVE come that they may have life, and have it in abundance. —Jn 10:10

A reason to believe

REFLECTION. For those who don't know Christ and His forgiveness, understanding who He is and why He came can be confusing. Many people have divergent opinions on who He is.

Jesus makes it clear as to why He came. He desires that all people experience His love and enjoy an abundant life. How can you help others come to the true knowledge of who He is?

PRAYER. *St. Joseph, assist me in my desire to articulate who Jesus is to others.*

 O ONE takes it away from me. I lay it down of my own free will. —Jn 10:18

Constant sacrifice

REFLECTION. Hollywood has some ideas about manhood which are on display on the big screen. The "male hero" is usually one who takes control, acts alone, and has little to do with a wife or children.

Catholic men model Jesus who laid down His life for the sake of others. Which model do you follow? Hollywood or Christ?

PRAYER. *Lord God, may You be my model for how I live my life each day.*

Y SHEEP listen to my voice; I know them, and they follow me.

—Jn 10:27

Whose voice do you listen to?

REFLECTION. When shepherds take the sheep they are entrusted with to pasture they inevitably meet other shepherds with their flocks. The sheep mingle and because sheep look alike it is difficult to discern whose sheep are whose.

The key is in the shepherd's voice. He only needs to speak or sing and his sheep separate from the others and follow him. How do you discern Jesus' voice today?

PRAYER. *Jesus, the Good Shepherd, attune my ears and heart to Your voice.*

ND Jesus began to weep. —Jn 11:35

DEC. 17

His grief poured down His face

REFLECTION. In most translations of scripture, John 11:35 is the shortest verse. It gives us a glimpse into the heart of Jesus and how He feels when His children are grieving. Jesus truly has empathy for those who are suffering.

Do we allow our hearts to be moved with compassion?

PRAYER. *Compassionate Lord, forgive me for my callousness towards those who suffer.*

THIS is how everyone will know that you are my disciples: if you love one another —Jn 13:35

DEC. 18

Love in action is the measure

REFLECTION. During sports playoffs people love to wear the jerseys and hats of their favorite teams and post away on social media. They are identifying with their team.

As Catholics, sacred jewelry and social media posts can point to who and what we believe. They are not a substitute however for action and Christian love. At the end of our lives we will be judged by love.

PRAYER. *Jesus our Messiah, may my life be marked by love in word and action.*

WHOEVER abides in me, and I in him, will bear much fruit. —Jn 15:5

DEC. 19

Stay connected

REFLECTION. The words *abide* and *remain* appear twelve times in the beginning of the fifteenth chapter of John. The sheer repetition of this word should signal to us the importance of staying connected to Jesus.

A branch broken or separated from the tree cannot bear fruit and men separated from Christ will do the same. How do you "abide in Him" each day?

PRAYER. *Jesus the True Vine, may nothing separate me from You all my days.*

O ANANIAS went and entered the house. He laid his hands on Saul and said, "Brother Saul." —Acts 9:17

**DEC.
20**

A brother won over

REFLECTION. The conversion of Saul is depicted by many artists throughout the ages. Saul, who would be renamed Paul, encountered the risen Lord and His life was forever changed.

Ananias would be used by God to pray over Paul and treat him as a brother despite his past. Catholic men, too, should never judge another's past but see Christ who lives in them.

PRAYER. *Lord Jesus, use me as You did Ananias to open another's eyes to who You are.*

 F IN speaking I use human and angelic tongues but do not have love, I am nothing more than a noisy gong or a clanging symbol. —1 Cor 13:1

**DEC.
21**

Activity without accomplishment

REFLECTION. The city of Corinth was the brass-making capital of the ancient world. Imagine shop after shop of artisans pounding on the brass as they shaped it and molded it. It must have been a deafening environment to work in.

St. Paul was well aware of this and writes to the Corinthian community that without love our words are just clatter. Loving words need loving actions.

PRAYER. *Loving Lord, as Your words were backed up by actions may I do the same.*

ECAUSE of his boundless love, Jesus became what we are that he might make us to be what he is. —St. Irenaeus

God's gift of self

REFLECTION. The season of Advent gives us opportunities to ponder the incarnation of God in the person of Jesus. The songs, the prayers, and the liturgy all direct us to that little town of Bethlehem where God became man.

The gift of God is ever unfolding in our own lives as we continue to reveal the grace of God and become gifts to others.

PRAYER. *Mary and Joseph, pray for me as I prepare to receive your Son ever more fully.*

 T IS Christmas every time you let God love others through you. —St. Teresa of Calcutta

Anticipating Christ

REFLECTION. Welcoming Jesus on Christmas morning is a memory that many carry from their childhood into old age. Mother Teresa reminds us that every time we love, Christ is born anew in and through us.

The awakening of Christ in others is not reserved for one day, but what a joy that we can bring His love many times each day. Prepare for Christmas through opening your heart to others.

PRAYER. *Come Lord Jesus, may we who have encountered Jesus share that love with all.*

DVENT'S intention is to awaken the most profound and basic emotional memory within us, the memory of the God who became a child.

DEC.
24

—Pope Benedict XVI

Open hearts

REFLECTION. Memory is a beautiful thing for it can take us instantly to foreign lands and previous moments in our lives that were filled with great joy or perhaps sadness.

Christmas Eve sets our sights and sounds to the greatest memory known to man which was when God became man. Take some time to ponder this great mystery.

PRAYER. *My God, how wondrously awesome it is that You love us and came to show us in person.*

 E IS the image of the invisible God, the firstborn of all creation. —Col 1:15

DEC.
25

God became one of us

REFLECTION. Christmas morning is unlike any other day of the year. Childhood memories of presents, family, and celebrations flood the mind as these traditions are replicated for our own children.

The greatest gift of course is not under the tree but in the manger—God's outward sign that we are remembered, that we are loved, and that we are worth being redeemed in our Father's eyes.

PRAYER. *Praise You Father, for You have redeemed the world and revealed Your face of love.*

MAKE the family of Nazareth a model for every home. —St. John Paul II

DEC. 26

The domestic church

REFLECTION. The Holy Family of Nazareth welcomed a child both into the world and into a home. Each family member plays a role in building a community of love in the home. The larger the family the greater the sacrifice needed to serve the needs of the rest.

As St. Joseph displayed protective love for his wife and child so must men continue to love and serve their family.

PRAYER. *St. Joseph, pray that I may be an example of love and service to my "holy" family.*

TAKE home this Word of Jesus, carry it in your hearts, share it with the family. —Pope Francis

DEC. 27

At home with Jesus

REFLECTION. There can be a temptation to leave the infant Jesus in the manger. We celebrate Christmas and move on to the next thing.

Jesus desires that His life, death, and Resurrection continue to bring meaning to your life. For that to happen you must stay connected in faith each day. Jesus comes as an infant but desires your faith to grow into an adult faith.

PRAYER. *Living Lord, may You continue to grow in me so I may be more like You.*

187

Y THE way we have lived our lives, we have represented or misrepresented God to people. —Msgr. James Turro

DEC. 28

A witness for Christ

REFLECTION. When a child is born visiting friends and family will say something like: "Oh, he has his father's eyes!" We take these affirmations as compliments and look for the resemblance in other areas too.

As Catholic men we are called to represent Christ in our words and actions.

PRAYER. *St. Joseph, assist me in representing Jesus to others, especially to those who don't know Him.*

 HUS, the Gospel is not simply about Jesus Christ. The Gospel is Jesus Christ. He is the final revelation of God. —Bishop Arthur J. Serratelli

DEC. 29

The first and last word

REFLECTION. It's impossible to separate the message from the messenger when speaking about Jesus Christ. Jesus did not come to bring about a new moral code or to show us a way.

Jesus Christ is the way, the truth, and the life. Catholics do a great disservice by withholding our faith in Jesus from others. We are not merely part of a parish, we are part of the body of Christ.

PRAYER. *Lord God, may I never be shy in proclaiming Jesus as Lord and Savior.*

E HAVE all known the long lone-liness, and we have found the answer is community.
—Dorothy Day

DEC. 30

We are one body in Christ

REFLECTION. Dorothy Day served the poor in Manhattan's lower East side beginning in the 1930s. Her journey to Catholicism took many twists and turns, heartaches, and failures. One lesson she learned is that we were made for community.

Are your eyes and ears open to those who don't have community? Will you share the joy you've found in the Christian community?

PRAYER. *Mary, help me to include others who are longing for love and community.*

ELL, I got there in the end with the help of many friends. Some who helped by simply just believing.
—Jake Burns

DEC. 31

A new year awaits

REFLECTION. At the end of each year we tend to take stock of the previous year and what possi-bilities lay ahead in the new. The important thing to remember is that God goes with us each step of the way.

At the end of our days, when we meet God face to face, hopefully we will have heaven as our reward, and we will greet those whom we've helped along the way.

PRAYER. *Almighty God, may this New Year be filled with opportunities to share Your peace.*

To You, O Blessed Joseph

TO YOU, O blessed Joseph,
do we come in our tribulation,
and having implored the help of your most holy
   spouse,
we confidently invoke your patronage also.
Through that charity which bound you
to the immaculate Virgin Mother of God
and through the paternal love
with which you embraced the Child Jesus,
we humbly beg you graciously to regard
the inheritance that Jesus Christ has purchased by
   His Blood,
and with your power and strength to aid us in our
   necessities.
O most watchful Guardian of the Holy Family,
defend the chosen children of Jesus Christ;
O most loving father,
ward off from us every contagion of error and cor-
   rupting influence;
O our most mighty protector,
be propitious to us and from heaven assist us
in our struggle with the power of darkness;
and, as once you rescued the Child Jesus from
   deadly peril,
so now protect God's Holy Church
from the snares of the enemy and from all adver-
   sity;
shield, too, each one of us by your constant protection,
so that, supported by your example and your aid,
we may be able to live piously,
to die holy,
and to obtain eternal happiness in heaven. Amen.

Prayer to Discern God's Plan
Made Known in Everyday Life

LORD Jesus Christ,
You came to earth and had an immeasurable effect
on the lives of those whom You met.
Let me realize that Your Father works
through people I meet every day of my life.
In every encounter and in every event,
You are coming to meet me—
if only I can discern Your presence.
And by my own life I also become for others
a bearer of God's plan.
Help me to respond to Your call gladly
when it comes to me each day in others.

Prayer of Fathers

HEAVENLY Father,
You have been pleased to let me be called
by the name that is Yours from all eternity.
Help me to be worthy of that name.
May I always be for my children a source of
    life—
corporal, intellectual, and spiritual.
Enable me to contribute in great part
to their physical growth by my work,
to their mental advancement by good schooling
and to their supernatural life by my prayer and
    example,
so that they may become complete human
    beings
and true children of their heavenly Father.
Let me be conscious that my actions

are far more important than my words.
May I always give my children a good example
in all the situations of life.
May I wear my successes modestly,
and may my failures find me undaunted;
may I be temperate in time of joy
and steadfast in time of sorrow.
May I remain humble after doing good
and contrite after doing evil.
Above all, may I scrupulously respect
my children's rights as human persons
and their freedom to follow a rightly formed con-
        science,
while at the same time fulfilling my duty to guide
        them
in the way given us by Your Son Jesus.

Prayer for Friends

LORD Jesus Christ,
while on earth You had close and devoted
friends, such as John, Lazarus, Martha, and
        Mary.
You showed in this way that friendship is one of
        life's greatest blessings.
Thank You for the friends that You have given me
to love me in spite of my failures and weak-
        nesses,
and to enrich my life after Your example.
Let me ever behave toward them
as You behaved toward Your friends.
Bind us close together in You
and enable us to help one another on our earth-
        ly journey.

OTHER OUTSTANDING CATHOLIC BOOKS

INTRODUCTION TO A DEVOUT LIFE—Adapted by Sr. Halcon J. Fisk. St. Francis de Sales reached out to everyone through this small book, showing that devotion is available to everyone in every walk of life and occupation. **No. 163**

DAY BY DAY WITH ST. JOSEPH—By Msgr. Joseph Champlin and Msgr. Ken Lasch. Pray with St. Joseph every day with a Scripture verse, short reflection, and prayer. **No. 162**

DAILY MEDITATIONS ON GOD'S LOVE—By Marci Alborghetti. These Scripture verses, brief meditations, and prayers for each day of the year are all focused on God's love for us and praying with them every day will help us to make the sometimes difficult decision to love. 192 pages. **No. 183**

WORDS OF COMFORT FOR EVERY DAY—By Rev. Joseph T. Sullivan. Short meditation for every day, including a Scripture text and a meditative prayer to God the Father. Printed in two colors. 192 pages. **No. 186**

MARY DAY BY DAY—Introduction by Rev. Charles G. Fehrenbach, C.SS.R. Minute meditations for every day of the year, including a Scripture passage, a quotation from the Saints, and a concluding prayer. Printed in two colors with over 300 illustrations. **No. 180**

UPLIFTING THOUGHTS FOR EVERY DAY—By Rev. John Catoir. We can eliminate negative thinking and improve our emotional life by filling our mind with uplifting thoughts. 192 pages. **No. 197**

BIBLE DAY BY DAY—By Rev. John C. Kersten, S.V.D. Minute Bible meditations for every day, including a short Scripture text and brief reflection. Printed in two colors with 300 illustrations. **No. 150**

LIVING WISDOM FOR EVERY DAY—By Rev. Bennet Kelley, C.P. Choice texts from St. Paul of the Cross, one of the true masters of spirituality, and a prayer for each day. **No. 182**

MINUTE MEDITATIONS FOR EACH DAY—By Rev. Bede Naegele, O.C.D. This very attractive book offers a short Scripture text, a practical reflection, and a meaningful prayer for each day of the year. **No. 190**

catholicbookpublishing.com

See more titles now.

ISBN 978-1-941243-94-7

90000